OLD MOORE'S

HOROSCOPE
AND ASTRAL
DIARY

•

VIRGO

D1742607

foulsham
LONDON • NEW YORK • TORONTO • SYDNEY

foulsham

The Publishing House, Bennetts Close,
Cippenham, Berks SL1 5AP

ISBN 0-572-02244-1

Printed in Great Britain at
Cox & Wyman Ltd, Reading

CONTENTS

OLD MOORE'S HOROSCOPE AND ASTRAL DIARY

Old Moore's Horoscope and Astral Diary represents a major departure from the usual format of publications dedicated to popular Sun-sign astrology. In this book, more attention than ever before has been focused on the discovery of the 'real you', through a wealth of astrological information, presented in an easy to follow and interesting form, and designed to provide a comprehensive insight into your fundamental nature.

The interplay of the Sun and Moon form complex cycles that are brought to bear on each of us in different ways. In the pages that follow I will explain how a knowledge of these patterns in your life can make relationships with others easier and general success more possible. Realising when your mind and body are at their most active or inactive, and at what times your greatest efforts are liable to see you winning through, can be of tremendous importance. In addition, your interaction with other zodiac types is explored, together with a comprehensive explanation of your Sun-sign nature.

In the Astral Diary you will discover a day-to-day reading covering a fifteen-month period. The readings are compiled from solar, lunar and planetary relationships as they bear upon your own zodiac sign. In addition, easy-to-follow graphic charts offer you at a glance an understanding of the way that your personal life-cycles are running; what days are best for maximum effort and when your system is likely to be regenerating.

Because some people want to look deeper into the fascinating world of personal astrology, there is a section of the book allowing a more in-depth appraisal of the all-important zodiac sign that was 'Rising' at the time of your birth. You can also look at your own personal 'Moon Sign' using simple to follow instructions to locate the position of this very significant heavenly body on the day that you were born.

From a simple-to-follow diary section, on to an intimate understanding of the ever-changing child of the solar system that you are, my Horoscope and Astral Diary will allow you to unlock potential that you never even suspected you had.

With the help and guidance of the following pages, Old Moore wishes you a happy and prosperous future.

HERE'S LOOKING AT YOU

A ZODIAC PORTRAIT OF VIRGO
(24th AUGUST - 23rd SEPTEMBER)

Virgo is invariably recognised as being an orderly, neat, tidy and well co-ordinated sign, its subjects are thought of as being the sort of people who won't have a single hair out of place. Even something as innocuous as stains on clothing are said to send the typical Virgoan into a blind panic, so fastidious are these people supposed to be concerning every detail. Of course, as with every other zodiac sign there are Virgoans and Virgoans, though it has to be said that there is more than a grain of truth is this description of Mercury's Earth-sign rulership.

In terms of physical stature, the typical Virgo is likely to be medium in height, with an oval face, clear complexion and especially striking eyes, often bluish in colour. The nose is small and aquiline and the smile radiates a genuine sincerity.

But what about the person behind the looks, what really makes you tick as an individual? Being an Earth-sign individual, your outlook on life is likely to be rather conservative. It is important for you to present the right impression in public, so that you have a preference for dressing well. You are good in conversation, ruled as you are by that lord of communication, Mercury, and yet like all Earth-signs you have a basic quietness of nature that is as likely to see you choosing the written word, in place of the spoken one, for your most intimate considerations.

Although you are fairly robust in health, you do have a rather dodgy nervous system, a fact that means you need to take plenty of rest. Retreating into the countryside is ideal for you at times of stress. All too often however you keep pushing and striving for those objectives that you have set your mind on, a fact that sets you apart as being quite stubborn, and one that can lead to nervous exhaustion if you do not exercise care. Despite your generally rude good health, you can be something of a hypochondriac and take an interest in all matters of health and hygiene. Anxiety shown concerning the least ailment only serves to make you burn up yet more nervous energy, and can lead in itself to bouts of illness.

THE INTENTION

You must have been told just how particular Virgo subjects can be, even to the point of being over-critical. At your worst, you are a nitpicker, and this can give the impression that you think yourself to be perfect. In reality, you attempt to establish order in what you view as being a generally chaotic world, and to make all things work in a practical way. Your work is never done, at least that is how it appears to you; and in addition to the need to roll up your sleeves and get stuck into jobs personally, being ruled by Mercury, you also have a wealth of ideas about everything, and no lack of words to communicate them to the world at large. Whilst Gemini (Mercury's other rulership) wants information for its own sake, Virgoans seek to put it to practical use. As a result, others rely on you, and more often than not you are willing to shoulder the burden.

Because Virgo is a mutable sign, there is a suggestion of adaptability. This shows in terms of your ability to fit into existing situations, even if later you have to turn them round to your own point of view. It can seem that you will even seek to improve those situations that are doing quite well left to their own devices and 'Leave it alone' may be an instruction to carry around in your subconscious, if you don't want to upset people who think they are fine as they are. It isn't really your fault; you need to find order and appropriateness in all aspects of your everyday world. Yours is a restless and highly-strung sign, but one that possesses great determination, courage and compassion. You are dutiful. diligent and basically very kind.

YOUR VIRTUES

Those people who know you the best and on upon whom you have bestowed your life-long friendship would have no difficulty finding ways to extol your virtues, after all, are you not always around to help and advise when they need you the most? This is the sort of situation when you show yourself in the best light possible, because you are a born organiser and love to be of assistance. You are often to be found in the background, and don't need to be leading from the front, as would be the case with a Leo or a Sagittarian; and yet your influence in all you undertake is easily felt.

In your efforts to help the world, as well as yourself because nobody can be entirely altruistic, you show diplomacy, tact and shrewdness. On most occasions you act with forethought and do not know the meaning of defeat once your mind is made up. On the way, you avariciously hoover up all the information about life that comes your way, putting each and every fact to good use sooner or later. Anything and everything is grist to the mill of knowledge that grinds away constantly inside your mind. Virgoans are at their best in an occupation which allows full use of the mental faculties at their disposal, yet because the sign of the Virgin is of the Earth element, it is not unusual to find individuals from this part of the zodiac tilling the good earth for a living, or at least tending a flower bed at the weekends.

Perhaps your greatest virtue, and it is one that many astrologers leave out, is your ingenuity, which together with a good intuitive quality and the ability to work hard , can see you building a secure and stable position in life for yourself.

YOUR VICES

It is the essence of the universe that for every plus, there must be a minus. Astrology, like everything else, conforms to this principle, and nowhere is it better exemplified than in the mentally-motivated but loamy depths of Virgo. Let's face it; at your worst you can be tedious and argumentative, interfering and downright bloody-minded. It isn't that you set out to be this way, it's simply a natural consequence of your need to see everything running smoothly. The problem is that in your heart of hearts you don't really believe that anyone else can do things as well as you can. Because you have a natural tendency to gather around you the sort of people that either need your personal brand of 'help', or at least individuals who have observed and felt your kind heart, all is usually well. The problems arise when, as a natural consequence of living in a world full of other people, you come across those infuriating types who think they know better than you do. Woe betide them, because once you decide to dig your heels in, you can be as stubborn as a mule and as tenacious as a bulldog. All the same, you can be a little unreasonable yourself on occasions and so perhaps a bit more patience on your part would not be a bad thing.

Your nervous system is always working overtime, a fact that can be responsible for uncharacteristic displays of surly bad temper, particularly if you happen to think there is something physically wrong with you, which is quite often. This is when you really come into your own, worrying away at a particular point until everyone around flees from the room in frustration or anger. Take heart though; the whole world knows that underneath it all you have a heart as big as a bus, and they won't bear a grudge - even if you sometimes do!

LIVING A HAPPY LIFE

In your case there are a few definite pointers, the observation of which, whilst not guaranteed to make you rich or famous, could easily lead to a more contented existence. First of all, remember that you are what you eat. The happiest Virgoans seem to be those that avoid animal based products as much as possible; the simpler the fare, the better, seems to be the motto. This stems from the fact that you are born under the Earth element, indicating that the produce of the earth suits your constitution best. Born as you were in the late summer, the fruits of nature's larder have a particular part to play in keeping you healthy. And once you have your diet right, you next need to build a world where worries are kept to a minimum. Remember that your aspirations can be out of tune with your needs and that today's boredom can be tomorrow's security. In other words, what you want out of life may not be the same as what you need.

Get plenty of outdoor exercise, looking at nature, and climbing hills as often as you can. Too often, Virgoans are inclined to stay close to home, which may suit your retreatist tendencies but does nothing towards allowing you the communication that is so important in keeping you healthy from a mental point of view. When you are forced to stay close to your abode, cultivate as wide a circle of friends as you can manage and learn to accept each of them for what they are, interfering in their lives only when you are asked. It isn't that you mean to take people over, merely that you are just so much more organised than they are.

Make certain that there is always something going on to stimulate your active, busy mind; an association with societies or social groups is good. You can be of great use to others, with your verbal dexterity and organising skills, so that any charity would probably be grateful to have you around. But above all, remember that you are not half so confident regarding yourself as you sometimes give the impression of being. Learn to laugh at your own faults and you will like yourself a whole lot better.

WHAT'S RISING

YOUR RISING SIGN AND PERSONALITY

Perhaps you have come across this term 'Rising Sign' when looking at other books on astrology and may have been somewhat puzzled as to what it actually means. To those not accustomed to astrological jargon it could sound somewhat technical and mysterious, though in fact, in terms of your own personal birth chart, it couldn't be simpler. The Rising Sign is simply that part of the zodiac occupying the eastern horizon at the time of your birth. Because it is a little more difficult to discover than your sun-sign, many writers of popular astrology have tended to ignore it, which is a great shame, because, together with the Sun, your Rising Sign is the single most important factor in terms of setting your personality. So much so, that no appraisal of your astrological nature could be complete without it.

Your Rising Sign, also known as your 'Ascendant' or 'Ascending Sign' plays a great part in your looks - yes, astrology can even predict what you are going to be like physically. In fact, this is a very interesting point, because there appears to be a tie- in between astrology and genetics. Professional Astrologers for centuries have noted the close relationship that often exists between the astrological birth chart of parents and those of their offspring, so that, if you look like your Mother or Father, chances are that there is a close astrological tie-up. Rising signs especially appear to be handed down through families.

The first impression that you get, in an astrological sense, upon meeting a stranger, is not related to their sun-sign but to the zodiac sign that was rising at the moment they came into the world. The Rising Sign is particularly important because it modifies the way that you display your Sun-sign to the world at large. A good example of this might be that of Britain's best- known ex- Prime minister, Margaret Thatcher. This dynamic and powerful lady is a Libran by Sun-sign placing, indicating a light-hearted nature, pleasure loving and very flexible. However, Mrs Thatcher has Scorpio as her Rising Sign, bringing a steely determination and a tremendous capacity for work. It also bestows an iron will and the power to thrive under pressure.

WHAT'S RISING?

Here lies the true importance of the Rising Sign, for Mr Thatcher almost certainly knows a woman who most other people do not. The Rising Sign is a protective shell, and not until we know someone quite well do we start to discover the Sun-sign nature that hides within this often tough outer coat of astrological making. Your Rising Sign also represents your basic self-image, the social mask that is often so useful; and even if you don't think that you conform to the interpretation of your Ascendant, chances are that other people will think that you do.

The way that an individual looks, walks, sits and generally presents themselves to the world is all down to the Rising Sign. For example, a person possessed of Gemini Rising is apt to be very quick, energetic in all movements, deliberate in mannerisms and with a cheerful disposition. A bearer of a Taurean Ascendant on the other hand would probably not be so tall, more solid generally, quieter in aspect and calmer in movement. Once you come to understand the basics of astrology it is really very easy to pick out the Rising Signs of people that you come across, even though the Sun-sign is often more difficult to pin down. Keep an eye open for the dynamic and positive Aries Rising individual, or the retiring, shy but absolutely magnetic quality of of the Piscean Ascendant. Of course, in astrology, nothing is quite that simple. The position of a vast array of heavenly bodies at the time of birth also has to be taken into account, particularly that of the Moon and the inner planets Mercury and Venus. Nevertheless a knowledge of your Rising sign can be an invaluable aid in getting to know what really makes you tick as an individual.

To ascertain the exact degree of your Rising sign takes a little experience and recourse to some special material. However, I have evolved a series of tables that will enable you to discover at a glance what your Rising Sign is likely to be. All you need to know is the approximate time of your birth. At the back of the book you will find the necessary table related to your Sun-sign. Simply look down the left-hand column until you find your approximate time of birth, am or pm. Now scan across the top of the table to the place where your date of birth is shown. Look for the square where the two pieces of information connect and there is your Rising Sign. Now that you know what your Rising Sign is, read on, and learn even more about the fascinating interplay of astrological relationship.

VIRGO WITH VIRGO RISING

A doubling up of the qualities of Virgo is a very powerful package indeed and indicates to the world 'what you see is what you get.' This means that all the typical gains and losses of the Virgo incarnation are yours for the taking. You look after your own affairs very well, and probably everyone else's too. In love you are ardent and sincere and most people should have a very good idea of what to expect from you. Mentality is your motivating factor and that busy, inquisitive mind of yours is constantly on the go, searching for new material that you can assimilate into your life.

Now this is where choice comes in. Have you ever seen the television comedy series where the actress, Patricia Routledge plays the indefatigable Mrs Bucket? Here is the sign of Virgo at it's worst. Snobbish, house proud to the point of absurdity, interfering, calculating and over-anxious about impressions. If you choose one side of the fence, here is your role-model. Should you desire to come down on the other side however, you can opt instead for a steady, interesting life; anxious to serve when you can and happy to accept the rest of humanity for what it is. The choice is yours!

VIRGO WITH LIBRA RISING

Hardly the typical Virgo subject, you are much more likely to exude the qualities of your rising sign Libra. This is a happy combination, for whilst Virgo is inclined to take itself a little too seriously on occasions, Libra is fun loving, easy going, extravagant and certainly more socially orientated than Virgo. With your disarming charm (and probably more than your fair share of good looks) you approach the world with great sensitivity to the needs of others

Your sense of identity comes from others, and you are very susceptible to what your friends and relatives have to say. In some ways this is an admirable thing, though you should also take time out for self-study, and for coming to terms with your own deeper self. There is an inherent confusion about socialising because Libra always wants to be with others, whilst Virgo is often happy to be alone. You do need to show the more assertive qualities that lie deep within your nature and to recognise that just a little of the loyalty that you show to others could be turned back in your own direction.

VIRGO WITH SCORPIO RISING

Here the Virgoan qualities of discrimination and rational analysis combine with Scorpio's powerful intuition to create an individual who does not miss a trick. It would be very rare for you to overlook the smallest detail. Nevertheless, the judgements that you make regarding others can sometimes be a little harsh. It has to be said that your first impressions are usually correct, but remember that even you can be wrong and that words, once uttered, cannot be unsaid. You are sensitive to the needs of others in a practical way, which is why so many of your astrological brothers and sisters work in the medical profession. In personal relationships you are passionate and faithful - occasionally too much for your own good. You may well have some very definite ideas about the world, particularly from a political point of view. In many respects you are the perfect humanitarian, just as long as humanity wants what you think is best for them. Like all Scorpio-tinged people, you don't take very kindly to opposition. However, such is your determination that you can do much good for yourself and the people whose lives you touch.

VIRGO WITH SAGITTARIUS RISING

Blessed with an abundant store of healthy optimism, there is little doubt that some of the more negative traits of the Virgo nature are tempered or even eradicated by the cocktail presented when Jupiter ruled Sagittarius is in the ascendant. You often look on the brighter side of life, always seeking to establish a positive way in which you can view things. Being adaptable and communicative, you are always willing to learn, can easily keep more than one occupation going and are quite good at convincing other people of your point of view.

It is true that you are always looking for some greater meaning to many of life's complexities, and others find you restless to have around on occasion. They always forgive you though because you can be relied upon to have something interesting to say on any occasion. Of course, under-pinning this devil-take-care attitude is the hard, realistic Virgo subject, which is why you are likely to be more successful than the typical Archer might be, though despite Virgo's presence, you can spread yourself too thinly on occasions and need to discover what you really ought to be doing with your life.

VIRGO WITH CAPRICORN RISING

A double helping of the Earth element, as with all other astrological possibilities, has its pluses and minuses. You certainly have the ability to actualise your desires through sheer hard work, determination and effort. It's possible for you to see through the fog of everyday concerns to the heart of almost any situation and to work out instinctively the best course of action to take. In addition you make a very firm friend and are extremely trustworthy.

One of the problems that you may encounter, is a tendency to take yourself, and possibly life as a whole, a little too seriously, running the risk of alienating yourself from much 'lighter' sorts of people, who in reality are exactly the folk that you need around you. Worry is something that you should learn to come to terms with, perhaps by cultivating the simple belief in tomorrow looking after its own problems and also by realising that you cannot change the nature of the world as a whole, no matter how hard you may try. You like to learn and to plan and it is important for you to keep on the move, constantly searching for your own El Dorado. Nobody should knock this side of your nature though, because you often find it!

VIRGO WITH AQUARIUS RISING

There is something a little unusual about this combination of signs, in fact it might be said that you are far from run of the mill yourself. You have your share of eccentric little quirks that others find difficult to understand. Despite this you are kind-hearted and willing to go to almost any lengths to be of assistance. With a genuine desire to see your fellow men and women prosper in their own lives, the presence of Aquarius in your make-up creates an altruistic and philanthropic nature. A problem here is that being so truthful about everything yourself, you are inclined to believe that the rest of humanity is the same, which is why you can be so frequently disappointed when you discover that they are not. Even this may not be too much of a let-down, considering that you are not the world's most emotionally motivated individual anyway. Your biggest problem may be when it comes to intimacy, because you are far happier to be skating over the surface of deep water, in addition to which you tend to subject everything in life to the sharp knife of rational intellect.

VIRGO WITH PISCES RISING

The positive aspects of this combination are born of your wonderful sensitivity to others and the sacrifices that you are willing to make on their behalf. Your kindness is laudable and you are usually willing to take others as you find them, not as you would wish them to be. All of this makes you a very popular person and it is only a pity that you cannot also be more discriminating and selective in your choice of friends and associates.

The secret seems to lie in distancing yourself from people and situations emotionally. Not an easy thing for you to do when guilt trips are the inevitable outcome. Because you are probably a fairly retiring type, there are occasions when you seem to be left at the starting post in practical matters, yet in personal relationships there are few to equal you and it is in this sphere of life that you really do come into your own. Even this can be a problem on occasions because you are inclined to 'cling' so you do need to keep track of your own identity and needs on the way.

VIRGO WITH ARIES RISING

In one respect at least, you are typical of the sign of Virgo; specifically in your desire to be constantly busy. This might be where the similarity ends however, since you are much more impatient than the Virgin is usually considered to be, in addition to manifesting a greater degree of brashness, courage and general force of character. You are a force to be reckoned with, holding the cool and methodical thinking of an Earth sign individual, backed up by all the power of the most dynamic of the Fire signs. There is little that you set your mind on that you cannot achieve, partly because you are realistic.

You can be guaranteed to have your say, and as far as work is concerned, you simply have to be left alone to get on with things in your own sweet way. Some people might consider that you are a bit of a 'know it all', and they would probably be right, because generally speaking you do! Watch out for a tendency to be rather too brusque for your own good, making a few enemies on the way, but remain proud of your scrupulous honesty and your ability to sort out any dilemma at a lightning speed.

VIRGO WITH TAURUS RISING

Despite this being a double helping of the Earth element, with Taurus Rising it is apt to play down some of the more hard-edged qualities of Virgo. The combination tends to throw up a nature that can be observed as being less highly-strung than the typical Virgoan might be and may replace this with a more sensually motivated character, quite typical of the Bull. Thus you may show a fondness for good food and drink, plenty of sleep and long hours spent in the luxury of a deep bath.

Creativity is important, and so is the need to shine in your own right. Aided by Virgo, you may show signs of being a potentially good writer, or through Taurus, a painter. Others are almost certain to sit up and take notice of the unique blend that these two signs tend to create and, superficially at least, you can give much back in terms of natural warmth and affection. Below the surface things might be different, because there is an inherent coldness that will need to be controlled on occasions. If anything, you can be a little too sensible, for your own good and that of the world at large.

VIRGO WITH GEMINI RISING

Mercury, the planet of communication, rules both these signs, so you have a double helping of the communication skills that are so much a part of your Sun-sign. Nobody with a Gemini Ascendant is going to take themselves as seriously as the typical Virgoan might and so there is a 'lightness' of nature in your make-up that gives you extra charisma. Your sense of humour and timing are second to none and it isn't at all difficult for you to make an impression. There are a multitude of acquaintances in your life, though probably only a handful of really close, personal friends.

The combination of Gemini's inspiration, quick thinking and verbal dexterity, together with Virgoan persistence and concentration is a magical mixture. This can assure you of the best of both worlds, for you possess a working knowledge of the world as a whole, though you can specialise quite successfully too. The breezy personality that everyone knows you for may well mask a much more sensitive core. Despite your sociability, you prefer others to come and visit you, in a home which may well reflect typical Virgo pride in surroundings.

VIRGO WITH CANCER RISING

The critical and somewhat analytical faculties of Virgo are slightly diminished and softened with this Rising Sign. The Cancerian side of you tends to accept people the way they are, without trying to change them in any way. You can be a typical Cancerian fuss-pot though, wanting to mother everyone and sort them out generally. Both signs feel they know what is best for other people. In reality, the world could do with more people of your sort; you would excel in the medical profession, or anywhere that you can serve human need.

In terms of personality it is possible that you are sometimes too shy for your own good, and you are also highly emotional. Like all Crabs you hide your true feeling behind a crusty shell and don't really care for people probing too much. You might make a good writer and would be great at critical analysis of any sort. It could be hard to keep your mind working in a genuinely logical way, but then you are so intuitive, you probably don't have to. Don't be ashamed to find so much tenderness within yourself. Remember that it is a gift to be shared with others.

VIRGO WITH LEO RISING

As with all Leo Rising people, it is your way to make a big impression on others, such is your warm, magnanimous, self-promoting nature. Most people would never guess that you are a Virgo, unless they get to know you very well. In fact the two signs don't really work together all that well, indicating that you may sometimes overdo the qualities of one sign, to the detriment of the other. An easy blend is rare, though when you do achieve it, the world can revel in the sunny and playful aspects of the Lion and the practical approach of Virgo. In an emergency you are second to none and in your approach to other people you are generous to a fault, even if it means going without something yourself.

Unpredictability is possibly your stumbling block, as it is to anyone ruled predominantly by Mercury. In your case the trait is more emphasised and some people will find it difficult to come to terms with you because of this slight flaw in your nature. You are a hard worker and can quite easily dedicate yourself to a career or a cause. Most of all, you hate being told what to do.

VIRGO
IN LOVE AND FRIENDSHIP

WANT TO KNOW HOW WELL YOU GET ON WITH OTHER ZODIAC SIGNS?

THE TABLES BELOW DEAL WITH LOVE AND FRIENDSHIP

THE MORE HEARTS THERE ARE AGAINST ANY SIGN OF THE ZODIAC, THE BETTER THE CHANCE OF CUPID'S DART SCORING A DIRECT HIT.

THE SMILES OF FRIENDSHIP DISPLAY HOW WELL YOU WORK OR ASSOCIATE WITH ALL THE OTHER SIGNS OF THE ZODIAC.

Sign	Love (Hearts)	Friendship (Smiles)
ARIES	♥ ♥ ♥ ♥	☺ ☺ ☺
TAURUS	♥ ♥ ♥ ♥ ♥	☺ ☺ ☺ ☺ ☺
GEMINI	♥ ♥ ♥	☺ ☺ ☺
CANCER	♥	☺ ☺
LEO	♥ ♥	☺ ☺ ☺
VIRGO	♥ ♥ ♥ ♥ ♥	☺ ☺ ☺ ☺
LIBRA	♥ ♥	☺ ☺
SCORPIO	♥ ♥ ♥	☺ ☺ ☺
SAGITTARIUS	♥ ♥ ♥	☺ ☺ ☺
CAPRICORN	♥ ♥ ♥ ♥ ♥	☺ ☺ ☺ ☺ ☺
AQUARIUS	♥ ♥	☺ ☺ ☺
PISCES	♥ ♥ ♥	☺ ☺

THE MOON AND YOUR DAY-TO-DAY LIFE

Look up at the sky on cloudless nights and you are almost certain to see the Earth's closest neighbour in space, engaged in her intricate and complicated relationship with the planet upon which we live. The Moon isn't very large, in fact only a small fraction of the size of the Earth, but it is very close to us in spatial terms, and here lies the reason why the Moon probably has more of a part to play in your day-to-day life than any other body in space.

It is fair to say in astrological terms that if the Sun and Planets represent the hour and minute hands regulating your character swings and mood changes, the Moon is a rapidly sweeping second hand, governing emotions especially, but touching practically every aspect of your life.

Although the Moon moves so quickly, and maintains a staggeringly complex orbital relationship with the Earth, no book charting the possible ups and downs of your daily life could be complete without some reference to lunar action. For this reason I have included a number of the more important lunar cycles that you can observe within your own life, and also give you the opportunity to discover which zodiac sign the Moon occupied when you were born. Follow the instructions below and you will soon have a far better idea of where astrological cycles come from, and the part they play in your life.

SUN MOON CYCLES

The first lunar cycle deals with the relationship that the Moon keeps with your Sun sign. I have made the fluctuations of this pattern easy for you to understand by means of a simple cyclic graph. It appears on the first page of each 'Your Month At A Glance', under the title 'Highs and Lows'. The graph displays the lunar cycle and you will soon learn to understand how its movements have a bearing on your level of energy and your abilities. Once you recognise the patterns, you can work within them, making certain that your maximum efforts are expounded at the most opportune time.

MOON AGE CYCLES

Looking at the second lunar pattern that helps to make you feel the way you do, day-to-day, involves a small amount of work on your part to establish how you slot into the rhythm. However, since Moon Age cycles are one of the most potent astrological forces at work in your life, the effort is more than worthwhile.

This cycle refers to the way that the date of your birth fits into the Moon Phase pattern. Because of the complex relationship of the Earth and the Moon, we see the face of the lunar disc change throughout a period of roughly one month. The time between one New Moon (this is when there is no Moon to be seen) to the next New Moon, is about 29 days. Between the two the Moon would have seemed larger each night until the lunar disc was Full; it would then start to recede back towards New again. We call this cycle the Moon Age Cycle and classify the day of the New Moon as day 0. Full Moon occurs on day 15 with the last day of the cycle being either day 28 or day 29, dependent on the complicated motions of the combined Earth and Moon.

If you know on what Moon Age Day you were born, then you also know how you fit into the cycle. You would monitor the changes of the cycle as more or less tension in your body, an easy or a strained disposition, good or bad temper and so forth. In order to work out your Moon Age Day follow the steps below:

STEP 1: Look at the two New Moon Tables on pages 23 and 24. Down the left hand column you will see every year from 1902 to 1994 listed, and the months of the year appear across the top. Where the year of your birth and the month that you were born coincide, the figure shown indicates the date of the month on which New Moon occurred.

STEP 2: You need to pick the New Moon that occurred prior to your day of birth, so if your birthday falls at the beginning of the month, you may have to refer to the New Moon from the previous month. Once you have established the nearest New Moon prior to your birthday, (and of course in the correct year), all you have to do is count forward to your birthday. (Don't forget that the day of the New Moon is classed as 0.) As an example, if your were born on March 22nd 1962, the last New Moon before your birthday would have occurred on 6th March 1962. Counting forward from 6 to 22 would mean that you were born on Moon Age Day 16. If your Moon Phase Cycle crosses the end of February, don't forget to check whether or not you were born in a Leap Year. If so you will have to compensate for that fact.

HOW TO USE MOON AGE DAYS

Once you know your Moon Age Day, you can refer to the Diary section of the book, because there, on each day of the year, you will see that the Moon Age Day is listed. The day in each cycle that conforms to your own Moon Age monthly birthday should find you in a positive and optimistic frame of mind Your emotions are likely to be settled and your thinking processes clear and concise. There are other important days that you will want to know about on this cycle, and to make matters simpler I have compiled an easy to follow table on pages 25 and 26. Quite soon you will get to know which Moon Age Days influence you, and how.

Of course Moon Age Cycles, although specific to your own date of birth, also run within the other astrological patterns that you will find described in this book. So, for example, if your Moon Age Day coincided with a particular day of the month, but everything else was working to the contrary, you might be wise to delay any particularly monumental effort until another, more generally favourable, day. Sometimes cycles run together and occasionally they do not; this is the essence of astrological prediction.

YOUR MOON SIGN

Once you have established on what Moon Age Day you were born, it isn't too difficult to also discover what zodiac sign the Moon occupied on the day of your birth. Although the Moon is very small in size compared to some of the solar system's larger bodies, it is very close indeed to the Earth and this seems to give it a special astrological significance. This is why there are many cycles and patterns associated with the Moon that have an important part to play in the lives of every living creature on the face of our planet, Of all the astrological patterns associated with the Moon that have a part to play in your life, none is more potent than those related to the zodiac position of the Moon at birth. Many of the most intimate details of your personal make-up are related to your Moon Sign, and we will look at these now.

HOW TO DISCOVER YOUR MOON SIGN

The Moon moves through each sign of the zodiac in only two to three days. It also has a rather complicated orbital relationship with the Earth; for these reasons it can be difficult to work out what your Zodiac Moon Sign is. However, having discovered your Moon Age Day you are half way towards finding your Moon Sign, and in order to do so, simply follow the steps below:

STEP 1: Make sure that you have a note of your date of birth and also your Moon Age Day.

STEP 2: Look at Zodiac Moon Sign Table 1 on page 27. Find the month of your birth across the top of the table, and your date of birth down the left. Where the two converge you will see a letter. Make a note of the letter that relates to you.

STEP 3: Now turn to Zodiac Moon Sign Table 2 on pages 28 and 30. Look for your Moon Age Day across the top of the tables and the letter that you have just discovered down the left side. Where the two converge you will see a zodiac sign. The Moon occupied this zodiac sign on the day of your birth.

PLEASE NOTE: The Moon can change signs at any time of the day or night, and the signs listed in this book are generally applicable for 12 noon on each day. If you were born near the start or the end of a particular Zodiac Moon Sign, it is worth reading the character descriptions of adjacent signs. These are listed pages 30 to 35. So much of your nature is governed by the Moon at the time of your birth that it should be fairly obvious which one of the profiles relates to you.

YOUR ZODIAC MOON SIGN EXPLAINED

You will find a profile of all Zodiac Moon Signs on pages 30 to 35, showing in yet another way astrology helps to make you into the individual that you are. In each month in the Astral Diary, in addition to your Moon Age Day, you can also discover your Zodiac Moon Sign birthday (that day when the Moon occupies the same zodiac sign as it did when you were born). At these times you are in the best position to be emotionally steady and to make the sort of decisions that have real, lasting value.

NEW MOON TABLE

YEAR	JAN	FEB	MAR	APR	MAY	JUN	JUL	AUG	SEP	OCT	NOV	DEC
1902	9	8	9	8	7	6	5	3	2	1/30	29	29
1903	27	26	28	27	26	25	24	22	21	20	19	18
1904	17	15	17	16	15	14	14	12	10	18	8	8
1905	6	5	5	4	3	2	2/31	30	28	28	26	26
1906	24	23	24	23	22	21	20	19	18	17	16	15
1907	14	12	14	12	11	10	9	8	7	6	5	5
1908	3	2	3	2	1/30	29	28	27	25	25	24	24
1909	22	20	21	20	19	17	17	15	14	14	13	12
1910	11	9	11	9	9	7	6	5	3	2	1	1/30
1911	29	28	30	28	28	26	25	24	22	21	20	20
1912	18	17	19	18	17	16	15	13	12	11	9	9
1913	7	6	7	6	5	4	3	2/31	30	29	28	27
1914	25	24	26	24	24	23	22	21	19	19	17	17
1915	15	14	15	13	13	12	11	10	9	8	7	6
1916	5	3	5	3	2	1/30	30	29	27	27	26	25
1917	24	22	23	22	20	19	18	17	15	15	14	13
1918	12	11	12	11	10	8	8	6	4	4	3	2
1919	1/31	-	2/31	30	29	27	27	25	23	23	22	21
1920	21	19	20	18	18	16	15	14	12	12	10	10
1921	9	8	9	8	7	6	5	3	2	1/30	29	29
1922	27	26	28	27	26	25	24	22	21	20	19	18
1923	17	15	17	16	15	14	14	12	10	10	8	8
1924	6	5	5	4	3	2	2/31	30	28	28	26	26
1925	24	23	24	23	22	21	20	19	18	17	16	15
1926	14	12	14	12	11	10	9	8	7	6	5	5
1927	3	2	3	2	1/30	29	28	27	25	25	24	24
1928	21	19	21	20	19	18	17	16	14	14	12	12
1929	11	9	11	9	9	7	6	5	3	2	1	1/30
1930	29	28	30	28	28	26	25	24	22	20	20	19
1931	18	17	19	18	17	16	15	13	12	11	9	9
1932	7	6	7	6	5	4	3	2/31	30	29	2	27
1933	25	24	26	24	24	23	22	21	19	19	17	17
1934	15	14	15	13	13	12	11	10	9	8	7	6
1935	5	3	5	3	2	1/30	30	29	27	27	26	25
1936	24	22	23	21	20	19	18	17	15	15	14	13
1937	12	11	12	12	10	8	8	6	4	4	3	2
1938	1/31	-	2/31	30	29	27	27	25	23	23	22	21
1939	20	19	20	19	19	17	16	15	13	12	11	10
1940	9	8	9	7	7	6	5	4	2	1/30	29	28
1941	27	26	27	26	26	24	24	22	21	20	19	18
1942	16	15	16	15	15	13	13	12	10	10	8	8
1943	6	4	6	4	4	2	2	1/30	29	29	27	27
1944	25	24	24	22	22	20	20	18	17	17	15	15
1945	14	12	14	12	11	10	9	8	6	6	4	4
1946	3	2	3	2	1/30	29	28	26	25	24	23	23
1947	21	19	21	20	19	18	17	16	14	14	12	12

NEW MOON TABLE

YEAR	JAN	FEB	MAR	APR	MAY	JUN	JUL	AUG	SEP	OCT	NOV	DEC
1948	11	9	11	9	9	7	6	5	3	2	1	1/30
1949	29	27	29	28	27	26	25	24	23	21	20	19
1950	18	16	18	17	17	15	15	13	12	11	9	9
1951	7	6	7	6	6	4	4	2	1	1/30	29	28
1952	26	25	25	24	23	22	23	20	29	28	27	27
1953	15	14	15	13	13	11	11	9	8	8	6	6
1954	5	3	5	3	2	1/30	29	28	27	26	25	25
1955	24	22	24	22	21	20	19	17	16	15	14	14
1956	13	11	12	11	10	8	8	6	4	4	2	2
1957	1/30	-	1/31	29	29	27	27	25	23	23	21	21
1958	19	18	20	19	18	17	16	15	13	12	11	10
1959	9	7	9	8	7	6	6	4	3	2/31	30	29
1960	27	26	27	26	26	24	24	22	21	20	19	18
1961	16	15	16	15	14	13	12	11	10	9	8	7
1962	6	5	6	5	4	2	1/31	30	28	28	27	26
1963	25	23	25	23	23	21	20	19	17	17	15	15
1964	14	13	14	12	11	10	9	7	6	5	4	4
1965	3	1	2	1	1/30	29	28	26	25	24	22	22
1966	21	19	21	20	19	18	17	16	14	14	12	12
1967	10	9	10	9	8	7	7	5	4	3	2	1/30
1968	29	28	29	28	27	26	25	24	23	22	21	20
1969	1 9	17	18	16	15	14	13	12	11	10	9	9
1970	7	6	7	6	6	4	4	2	1	1/30	29	28
1971	26	25	26	25	24	22	22	20	19	19	18	17
1972	15	14	15	13	13	11	11	9	8	8	6	6
1973	5	4	5	3	2	1/30	29	28	27	26	25	25
1974	24	22	24	22	21	20	19	17	16	15	14	14
1975	12	11	12	11	11	9	9	7	5	5	3	3
1976	1/31	29	30	29	29	27	27	25	23	23	21	21
1977	19	18	19	18	18	16	16	14	13	12	11	10
1978	9	7	9	7	7	5	5	4	2	2/31	30	29
1979	27	26	27	26	26	24	24	22	21	20	19	18
1980	16	15	16	15	14	13	12	11	10	9	8	7
1981	6	4	6	4	4	2	1/31	29	28	27	26	26
1982	25	23	24	23	21	21	20	19	17	17	15	15
1983	14	13	14	13	12	11	10	8	7	6	4	4
1984	3	1	2	1	1/30	29	28	26	25	24	22	22
1985	21	19	21	20	19	18	17	16	14	14	12	12
1986	10	9	10	9	8	7	7	5	4	3	2	1/30
1987	29	28	29	28	27	26	25	24	23	22	21	20
1988	19	17	18	16	15	14	13	12	11	10	9	9
1989	7	6	7	6	5	3	3	1/31	29	29	28	28
1990	26	25	26	25	24	22	22	20	19	18	17	17
1991	15	14	15	13	13	11	11	9	8	8	6	6
1992	4	3	4	3	2	1/30	29	28	26	25	24	24
1993	24	22	24	22	21	20	19	17	16	15	14	14
1994	11	10	12	11	10	9	8	7	5	5	3	2

MOON AGE QUICK REFERENCE TABLE

SIGNIFICANT MOON AGE DAYS

		+ Days	- Days	* Days
Y	0	4, 6, 12, 14, 19, 21, 25, 28	9, 16, 23	0
O	1	5, 7, 13, 15, 20, 22, 26, 29	10, 17, 24	1
U	2	0, 6, 8, 14, 16, 21, 23, 27	11, 18, 25	2
R	3	1, 7, 9, 15, 17, 22, 24, 28	12, 19, 26	3
	4	2, 8, 10, 16, 18, 23, 25, 29	13, 20, 27	4
O	5	0, 3, 4, 9, 11, 17, 19, 24, 26	14, 21, 28	5
W	6	1, 4, 5, 10, 12, 18, 20, 25, 27	5, 22, 29	6
N	7	2, 5, 11, 13, 19, 21, 26, 28	0, 16, 23	7
	8	3, 6, 12, 14, 20, 22, 27, 29	1, 17, 24	8
M	9	0, 4, 7, 13, 15, 21, 23, 28	2, 18, 25	9
O	10	1, 5, 8, 14, 16, 22, 24, 29	3, 19, 26	10
O	11	0, 2, 6, 9, 15, 17, 23, 25	4, 20, 27	11
N	12	1, 3, 7, 10, 16, 18, 24, 26	5, 21, 28	12
	13	2, 4, 8, 11, 17, 19, 25, 27	6, 22, 29	13
A	14	3, 5, 9, 12, 18, 20, 26, 28	0, 7, 23	14
G	15	4, 6, 10, 13, 19, 21, 27, 29	1, 8, 24	15
E	16	0, 5, 7, 11, 14, 20, 22, 28	2, 9, 25	16
	17	1, 6, 8, 12, 15, 21, 23, 29	3, 10, 26	17
D	18	0, 2, 7, 9, 13, 16, 22, 24	4, 11, 27	18
A	19	1, 3, 8, 10, 14, 17, 23, 25	5, 12, 28	19
Y	20	2,4, 9, 11, 15, 18, 24, 26	6, 13, 29	20
	21	3, 5, 10, 12, 16, 19, 25, 27	0, 7, 14	21
	22	4, 6, 11, 13, 17, 20, 26, 28	1, 8, 15	22
	23	5, 7, 12, 14, 18, 21, 27, 29	2, 9, 16	23
	24	0, 6, 8, 13, 15, 19, 22, 28	3, 10, 17	24
	25	1, 7, 9, 14, 16, 20, 23, 29	4, 11, 18	25
	26	0, 2, 8, 10, 15, 17, 21, 24,	5, 12, 19	26
	27	1, 3, 9, 11, 16, 18, 22, 25	6, 13, 20	27
	28	2, 4, 10, 12, 17, 19, 23, 26	7, 14, 21	28
	29	3, 5, 11, 13, 18, 20, 24, 27	8, 15, 22	29

MOON AGE QUICK REFERENCE TABLE

The table opposite will allow you to plot the significant days on the Moon Age Day Cycle and to monitor the way they have a bearing on your own life. You will find an explanation of the Moon Age Cycles on pages 20 - 22. Once you know your own Moon Age Day, you can find it in the left-hand column of the table opposite, To the right of your Moon Age Day you will observe a series of numbers; these appear under three headings. + Days, - Days and * Days.

If you look at the Diary section of the book, immediately to the right of each day and date, the Moon Age Day number is listed. The Quick Reference Table allows you to register which Moon Age Days are significant to you. For example: if your own Moon Age Day is 5, each month you should put a + in the Diary section against Moon Age Days 0, 3, 4, 9, 11, 17, 19, 24, and 26. Jot down a - against Moon Age Days 14, 21 and 28, and a * against Moon Age Day 5. You can now follow your own personal Moon Age Cycle every day of the year.

+ Days are periods when the Moon Age Cycle is in tune with your own Moon Age Day. At this time life should be more harmonious and your emotions are likely to be running smoothly. These are good days for making decisions.

- Days find the Moon Age Cycle out of harmony with your own Moon Age Day. Avoid taking chances at these times and take life reasonably steady. Confrontation would not make sense.

* Days occur only once each Moon Age Cycle, and represent your own Moon Age Day. Such times should be excellent for taking the odd chance and for moving positively towards your objectives in life. On those rare occasions where a * day coincides with your lunar high, you would really be looking at an exceptional period and could afford to be quite bold and adventurous in your approach to life.

MOON ZODIAC SIGN TABLE 1

	Month	Jan	Feb	Mar	Apr	May	Jun	Jul	Aug	Sep	Oct	Nov	Dec
	1	A	D	F	J	M	O	R	U	X	a	e	i
	2	A	D	G	J	M	P	R	U	X	a	e	i
	3	A	D	G	J	M	P	S	V	X	a	e	m
	4	A	D	G	J	M	P	S	V	Y	b	f	m
	5	A	D	G	J	M	P	S	V	Y	b	f	n
	6	A	D	G	J	M	P	S	V	Y	b	f	n
	7	A	D	G	J	M	P	S	V	Y	b	f	n
	8	A	D	G	J	M	P	S	V	Y	b	f	n
	9	A	D	G	J	M	P	S	V	Y	b	f	n
D	10	A	E	G	J	M	P	S	V	Y	b	f	n
A	11	B	E	G	K	M	P	S	V	Y	b	f	n
Y	12	B	E	H	K	N	Q	S	V	Y	b	f	n
	13	B	E	H	K	N	Q	T	V	Y	b	g	n
O	14	B	E	H	K	N	Q	T	W	Z	d	g	n
F	15	B	E	H	K	N	Q	T	W	Z	d	g	n
	16	B	E	H	K	N	Q	T	W	Z	d	g	n
T	17	B	E	H	K	N	Q	T	W	Z	d	g	n
H	18	B	E	H	K	N	Q	T	W	Z	d	g	n
E	19	B	E	H	K	N	Q	T	W	Z	d	g	n
	20	B	F	H	K	N	Q	T	W	Z	d	g	n
M	21	C	F	H	L	N	Q	T	W	Z	d	g	n
O	22	C	F	I	L	O	R	T	W	Z	d	g	n
O	23	C	F	I	L	O	R	T	W	Z	d	i	q
N	24	C	F	I	L	O	R	U	X	a	e	i	q
	25	C	F	I	L	O	R	U	X	a	e	i	q
	26	C	F	I	L	O	R	U	X	a	e	i	q
	27	C	F	I	L	O	R	U	X	a	e	i	q
	28	C	F	I	L	O	R	U	X	a	e	i	q
	29	C	-	I	L	O	R	U	X	a	e	i	q
	30	C	-	I	L	O	R	U	X	a	e	i	q
	31	D	i	I	-	O	-	U	X	-	e	-	q

MOON ZODIAC

LETTER

Moon Age Day	0	1	2	3	4	5	6	7	8	9	10	11	12	13
A	Ca	Aq	Aq	Aq	Pi	Pi	Ar	Ar	Ar	Ta	Ta	Ge	Ge	Ge
B	Aq	Aq	Aq	Pi	Pi	Ar	Ar	Ar	Ta	Ta	Ge	Ge	Ge	Cn
C	Aq	Aq	Pi	Pi	Ar	Ar	Ar	Ta	Ta	Ge	Ge	Ge	Cn	Cn
B	Aq	Pi	Pi	Pi	Ar	Ar	Ta	Ta	Ta	Ge	Ge	Cn	Cn	Le
E	Pi	Pi	Pi	Ar	Ar	Ta	Ta	Ta	Ge	Ge	Cn	Cn	Cn	Le
F	Pi	Pi	Ar	Ar	Ar	Ta	Ta	Ge	Ge	Cn	Cn	Cn	Le	Le
G	Pi	Ar	Ar	Ar	Ta	Ta	Ge	Ge	Ge	Cn	Cn	Le	Le	Le
H	Ar	Ar	Ar	Ta	Ta	Ge	Ge	Ge	Cn	Cn	Le	Le	Le	Vi
I	Ar	Ar	Ta	Ta	Ge	Ge	Ge	Cn	Cn	Cn	Le	Le	Vi	Vi
J	Ar	Ta	Ta	Ta	Ge	Ge	Cn	Cn	Cn	Le	Le	Vi	Vi	Vi
K	Ta	Ta	Ta	Ge	Ge	Cn	Cn	Cn	Le	Le	Vi	Vi	Vi	Li
L	Ta	Ta	Ge	Ge	Ge	Cn	Cn	Le	Le	Vi	Vi	Vi	Li	Li
M	Ta	Ge	Ge	Ge	Cn	Cn	Le	Le	Le	Vi	Vi	Li	Li	Li
N	Ge	Ge	Ge	Cn	Cn	Le	Le	Le	Vi	Vi	Li	Li	Li	Sc
O	Ge	Ge	Cn	Cn	Cn	Le	Le	Vi	Vi	Li	Li	Sc	Sc	Sc
P	Ge	Cn	Cn	Cn	Le	Le	Vi	Vi	Vi	Li	Li	Sc	Sc	Sc
Q	Cn	Cn	Cn	Le	Le	Vi	Vi	Li	Li	Sc	Sc	Sc	Sa	Sa
R	Cn	Cn	Le	Le	Le	Vi	Vi	Li	Li	Li	Sc	Sc	Sa	Sa
S	Cn	Le	Le	Le	Vi	Vi	Li	Li	Li	Sc	Sc	Sa	Sa	Sa
T	Le	Le	Le	Vi	Vi	Li	Li	Li	Sc	Sc	Sa	Sa	Sa	Ca
U	Le	Le	Vi	Vi	Li	Li	Li	Sc	Sc	Sa	Sa	Ca	Ca	Ca
V	Le	Vi	Vi	Vi	Li	Li	Sc	Sc	Sc	Sa	Sa	Ca	Ca	Ca
W	Le	Vi	Vi	Li	Li	Sc	Sc	Sa	Sa	Sa	Ca	Ca	Aq	Aq
X	Vi	Vi	Li	Li	Li	Sc	Sc	Sa	Sa	Sa	Ca	Ca	Aq	Aq
Y	Vi	Li	Li	Li	Sc	Sc	Sa	Sa	Sa	Ca	Ca	Aq	Aq	Aq
Z	Li	Li	Li	Sc	Sc	Sc	Sa	Sa	Ca	Ca	Ca	Aq	Aq	Pi
a	Li	Li	Li	Sc	Sc	Sa	Sa	Sa	Ca	Ca	Aq	Aq	Pi	Pi
b	Li	Li	Sc	Sc	Sa	Sa	Ca	Ca	Ca	Aq	Aq	Pi	Pi	Ar
d	Li	Sc	Sc	Sc	Sa	Sa	Ca	Ca	Ca	Aq	Aq	Pi	Pi	Pi
e	Sc	Sc	Sc	Sa	Sa	Ca	Ca	Aq	Aq	Aq	Pi	Pi	Ar	Ar
f	Sc	Sc	Sa	Sa	Ca	Ca	Aq	Aq	Pi	Pi	Ar	Ar	Ta	Ta
g	Sc	Sa	Sa	Ca	Ca	Aq	Aq	Pi	Pi	Pi	Ar	Ar	Ta	Ta
i	Sa	Sa	Ca	Ca	Ca	Aq	Aq	Pi	Pi	Ar	Ar	Ta	Ta	Ge
m	Sa	Sa	Ca	Ca	Aq	Aq	Aq	Pi	Pi	Ar	Ar	Ta	Ta	Ge
n	Sa	Ca	Ca	Aq	Aq	Pi	Pi	Ar	Ar	Ta	Ta	Ta	Ge	Ge
q	Ca	Ca	Aq	Aq	Pi	Pi	Ar	Ar	Ar	Ta	Ta	Ge	Ge	Ge

Ar = Aries Ta = Taurus Ge = Gemini Cn = Cancer Le = Leo Aq = Aquarius

SIGN TABLE 2

14	15	16	17	18	19	20	21	22	23	24	25	26	27	28	29
Cn	Cn	Le	Le	Le	Vi	Vi	Li	Li	Li	Sc	Sc	Sa	Sa	Sa	Ca
Cn	Le	Le	Le	Vi	Vi	Li	Li	Li	Sc	Sc	Sa	Sa	Sa	Ca	Ca
Le	Le	Le	Vi	Vi	Vi	Li	Li	Sc	Sc	Sc	Sa	Sa	Ca	Ca	Ca
Le	Le	Vi	Vi	Vi	Li	Li	Sc	Sc	Sc	Sa	Sa	Ca	Ca	Aq	Aq
Le	Vi	Vi	Vi	Li	Li	Sc	Sc	Sc	Sa	Sa	Ca	Ca	Aq	Aq	Aq
Vi	Vi	Vi	Li	Li	Li	Sc	Sc	Sa	Sa	Sa	Ca	Ca	Aq	Aq	Aq
Vi	Vi	Li	Li	Li	Sc	Sc	Sa	Sa	Sa	Ca	Ca	Aq	Aq	Aq	Pi
Vi	Li	Li	Li	Sc	Sc	Sa	Sa	Sa	Ca	Ca	Aq	Aq	Aq	Pi	Pi
Li	Li	Li	Sc	Sc	Sc	Sa	Sa	Ca	Ca	Ca	Aq	Aq	Pi	Pi	Pi
Li	Li	Sc	Sc	Sc	Sa	Sa	Ca	Ca	Ca	Aq	Aq	Pi	Pi	Pi	Ar
Li	Sc	Sc	Sc	Sa	Sa	Ca	Ca	Ca	Aq	Aq	Pi	Pi	Pi	Ar	Ar
Li	Sc	Sc	Sa	Sa	Sa	Ca	Ca	Aq	Aq	Aq	Pi	Pi	Ar	Ar	Ar
Sc	Sc	Sa	Sa	Sa	Ca	Ca	Aq	Aq	Aq	Pi	Pi	Ar	Ar	Ar	Ta
Sc	Sa	Sa	Sa	Ca	Ca	Aq	Aq	Aq	Pi	Pi	Ar	Ar	Ar	Ta	Ta
Sa	Sa	Sa	Ca	Ca	Ca	Aq	Aq	Pi	Pi	Pi	Ar	Ar	Ta	Ta	Ta
Sa	Sa	Ca	Ca	Ca	Aq	Aq	Pi	Pi	Pi	Ar	Ar	Ta	Ta	Ta	Ge
Sa	Ca	Ca	Ca	Aq	Aq	Pi	Pi	Pi	Ar	Ar	Ta	Ta	Ta	Ge	Ge
Sa	Ca	Ca	Aq	Aq	Aq	Pi	Pi	Ar	Ar	Ar	Ta	Ta	Ge	Ge	Ge
Ca	Ca	Aq	Aq	Aq	Pi	Pi	Ar	Ar	Ar	Ta	Ta	Ge	Ge	Ge	Cn
Ca	Aq	Aq	Aq	Pi	Pi	Ar	Ar	Ar	Ta	Ta	Ge	Ge	Ge	Cn	Cn
Aq	Aq	Aq	Pi	Pi	Pi	Ar	Ar	Ta	Ta	Ta	Ge	Ge	Cn	Cn	Cn
Aq	Aq	Pi	Pi	Pi	Ar	Ar	Ta	Ta	Ta	Ge	Ge	Cn	Cn	Cn	Le
Pi	Pi	Pi	Pi	Ar	Ar	Ta	Ta	Ta	Ge	Ge	Cn	Cn	Cn	Le	Le
Pi	Pi	Pi	Ar	Ar	Ar	Ta	Ta	Ge	Ge	Ge	Cn	Cn	Le	Le	Le
Pi	Pi	Ar	Ar	Ar	Ta	Ta	Ge	Ge	Ge	Cn	Cn	Le	Le	Le	Vi
Pi	Pi	Ar	Ar	Ar	Ta	Ta	Ge	Ge	Ge	Cn	Cn	Le	Le	Le	Vi
Ar	Ar	Ar	Ar	Ta	Ta	Ge	Ge	Ge	Cn	Cn	Cn	Le	Le	Vi	Vi
Ar	Ar	Ar	Ta	Ta	Ta	Ge	Ge	Cn	Cn	Cn	Le	Le	Vi	Vi	Vi
Ar	Ar	Ta	Ta	Ge	Ge	Ge	Cn	Cn	Cn	Le	Le	Vi	Vi	Vi	Li
Ta	Ta	Ta	Ge	Ge	Ge	Cn	Cn	Cn	Le	Le	Le	Vi	Vi	Li	Li
Ge	Ta	Ge	Ge	Ge	Cn	Cn	Cn	Le	Le	Le	Vi	Vi	Li	Li	Li
Ge	Ta	Ge	Ge	Cn	Cn	Cn	Le	Le	Le	Vi	Vi	Li	Li	Li	Sc
Ge	Ge	Ge	Cn	Cn	Cn	Le	Le	Vi	Vi	Vi	Li	Li	Sc	Sc	Sc
Ge	Ge	Cn	Cn	Cn	Le	Le	Le	Vi	Vi	Vi	Li	Li	Sc	Sc	Sa
Cn	Ge	Cn	Cn	Le	Le	Le	Vi	Vi	Vi	Li	Li	Sc	Sc	Sc	Sa
Cn	Cn	Cn	Le	Le	Le	Vi	Vi	Li	Li	Li	Sc	Sc	Sa	Sa	Sa

Vi = Virgo Li = Libra Sc = Scorpio Sa = Sagittarius Ca = Cancer
Pi = Pisces

MOON SIGNS

MOON IN ARIES

You have a strong imagination and a desire to do things in your own way. Showing no lack of courage you can forge your own path through life with great determination.

Originality is one of your most important attributes, you are seldom stuck for an idea though your mind is very changeable and more attention might be given over to one job at once. Few have the ability to order you around and you can be quite quick tempered. A calm and relaxed attitude is difficult for you to adopt but because you put tremendous pressure on your nervous system it is vitally important for you to forget about the cut and thrust of life from time to time. It would be fair to say that you rarely get the rest that you both need and deserve and because of this there is a chance that your health could break down from time to time.

Emotionally speaking you can be a bit of a mess if you don't talk to the folks that you are closest to and work out how you really feel about things. Once you discover that there are people willing to help you there is suddenly less necessity for trying to tackle everything yourself.

MOON IN TAURUS

The Moon in Taurus at the time you were born gives you a courteous and friendly manner that is likely to assure you of many friends.

The good things in life mean a great deal to you for Taurus is an Earth sign and delights in experiences that please the senses. This probably makes you a lover of good food and drink and might also mean that you have to spend time on the bathroom scales balancing the delight of a healthy appetite with that of looking good which is equally important to you.

Emotionally you are fairly stable and once you have opted for a set of standards you are inclined to stick to them because Taurus is a Fixed sign and doesn't respond particularly well to change. Intuition also plays an important part in your life.

MOON IN GEMINI

The Moon in the sign of Gemini gives a warm-hearted character, full of sympathy and usually ready to help those in difficulty. In some matters you are very reserved, whilst at other times you are articulate and chatty: this is part of the paradox of Gemini which always brings duplicity to the nature. The knowledge you possess of local and national affairs is very good, this strengthens and enlivens your intellect making you good company and endowing you with many friends. Most of the people with whom you mix have a high opinion of you and will stand ready to leap to your defence, not that this is generally necessary for although you are not martial by nature, you are more than capable of defending yourself verbally.

Travel plays an important part in your life and the naturally inquisitive quality of your mind allows you to benefit greatly from changes in scenery. The more you mix with people from different cultures and backgrounds the greater your interest in life becomes and intellectual stimulus is the meat and drink of the Gemini individual.

You can gain through reading and writing as well as the cultivation of artistic pursuits but you do need plenty of rest in order to avoid fatigue.

MOON IN CANCER

Moon in Cancer at the time of birth is a most fortunate position since the sign of Cancer is the Moon's natural home. This means that the qualities of compassion and understanding given by the Moon are especially enhanced in your nature and you cope quite well with emotional pressures that would bother others. You are friendly and sociably inclined. Domestic tasks don't really bother you and your greatest love is likely to be for home and family. Your surroundings are particularly important and you hate squalor and filth.

Your basic character, although at times changeable like the Moon itself, depends upon symmetry. Little wonder then that you are almost certain to have a love of music and poetry. Not surprising either that you do all within your power to make your surroundings comfortable and harmonious, not only for yourself, but on behalf of the folk who mean so much to you.

MOON IN LEO

You are especially ambitious and self-confident. The best qualities of both the Moon and the Sign of Leo come together here to ensure that you are warm-hearted and fair, characteristics that are almost certain to show through no matter what other planetary positions your chart contains.

You certainly don't lack the ability to organise, either yourself or those around you, and you invariably rise to a position of responsibility no matter what you decide to do with your life. Perhaps it is just as well because you don't enjoy being an 'also ran' and would much rather be an important part of a small organisation than a menial in a larger one.

In love you are likely to be lucky and happy provided that you put in that extra bit of effort and you can be relied upon to build comfortable home surroundings for yourself and also those for whom you feel a particular responsibility. It is likely that you will have a love of pleasure and sport and perhaps a fondness for music and literature. Life brings you many rewards, though most of them are as a direct result of the effort that you are able to put in on your own behalf. All the same you are inclined to be more lucky than average and will usually make the best of any given circumstance.

MOON IN VIRGO

This position of the Moon endows you with good mental abilities and a keen receptive memory. By nature you are probably quite reserved, nevertheless you have many friends, especially of the opposite sex, and you gain a great deal as a result of these associations. Marital relationships need to be discussed carefully and kept as harmonious as possible because personal attachments can be something of a problem to you if sufficient attention is not given to the way you handle them.

You are not ostentatious or pretentious, two characteristics that are sure to improve your popularity. Talented and persevering you possess artistic qualities and are a good home- maker. Earning your honours through genuine merit you can work long and hard towards your objectives but probably show very little pride in your genuine achievements. Many short journeys will be undertaken in your life.

MOON IN LIBRA

With the Moon in Libra you have a popular nature and don't find it particularly difficult to make friends. Most folk like you, probably more than you think, and all get together's would be more fun with you present. Libra, for all its good points, is not the most stable of Astrological signs and as a result your emotions can prove to be a little unstable too. Although the Moon in Libra is generally said to be good for love and marriage, the position of the Sun, and also the Rising Sign, in your own birth chart will have a greater than usual effect on your emotional and loving qualities.

You cannot live your life in isolation and must rely on other people, who are likely to play an important part in your decision making. Co-operation is crucial for you because Libra represents the 'balance' of life that can only be achieved through harmonious relationships. An offshoot of this fact is that you do not enjoy being disliked and, like all Lirans are a natural diplomat.

Conformity is not always easy for you, because Libra is an Air sign and likes to go its own way.

MOON IN SCORPIO

Some people might call you a little pushy, in fact all you really want to do is live your life to the full, and to protect yourself and your family from the pressures of life that you recognise all too readily. You should avoid giving the impression of being sarcastic or too impulsive, at the same time using your energies wisely and in a constructive manner.

Nobody could doubt your courage which is great, and you invariably achieve what you set out to do, by force of personality as well as by the effort that you are able to put in. You are fond of mystery and are probably quite perceptive as to the outcome of situations and events.

Problems can arise in your relationships with members of the opposite sex, so before you commit yourself emotionally it is very important to examine your motives carefully and ensure that the little demon, jealousy, always a problem with Scorpio positions, does not cloud your judgement in love matches. You need to travel and can make gains as a result.

MOON IN SAGITTARIUS

The Moon is Sagittarius helps to make you a generous individual with humanitarian qualities and a kind heart. Restlessness may be an endemic part of your character for your mind is seldom still. Perhaps because of this you have an overwhelming need for change that could lead you to several major moves during your adult life. You are probably a reasonably sporting sort of person and not afraid to stand your ground on the occasions when you know that you are correct in your judgement. What you have to say goes right to the heart of the matter and your intuition is very good.

At work you are quick and efficient in whatever you choose to do, and because you are versatile you make an ideal employee. Ideally you need work that is intellectually demanding because you are no drudge and would not enjoy tedious routines. In relationships you anger quickly if faced with stupidity or deception, though you are just as quick to forgive and forget. Emotionally there are times when you allow your heart rule your head.

MOON IN CAPRICORN

Born with the Moon in Capricorn, you are popular and may come into the public eye in one way or another. Your administrative ability is good and you are a capable worker. The watery Moon is not entirely at home in the Earth sign of Capricorn and as a result difficulties can be experienced, especially in the early years of life. Some initial lack of creative ability and indecision has to be overcome before the true qualities of patience and perseverance inherent in Capricorn can show through.

If caution is exercised in financial affairs you can accumulate wealth with the passing of time but you will always have to be careful about forming any partnerships because you are open to deception more than most. Under such circumstances you would be well advised to gain professional advice before committing yourself. Many people with the Moon in Capricorn take a healthy interest in social or welfare work. The organisational skills that you have, together with a genuine sympathy for others, means that you are ideally suited to this kind of career or pastime.

MOON IN AQUARIUS

With the Moon in Aquarius you are an active and agreeable person with a friendly easy going sort of nature. Being sympathetic to the needs of other people you flourish best in an easy going atmosphere. You are broad minded, just, and open to suggestion, though as with all faces of Aquarius the Moon here brings an unconventional quality that not everyone would find easy to understand.

You have a liking for anything strange and curious as well a fascination for old articles and places. Journeys to such locations would suit you doubly because you love to travel and can gain a great deal from the trips that you make. Political, scientific and educational work might all be of interest to you and you would gain from a career in some new and exciting branch of science or technology.

Money-wise, you make gains through innovation as much as by concentration and it isn't unusual to find Lunar Aquarians tackling more than one job at the same time. In love you are honest and kind.

MOON IN PISCES

This position assures you of a kind sympathetic nature, somewhat retiring at times but always taking account of others and doing your best to help them. As with all planets in Pisces there is bound to be some misfortunes on the way through life. In particular relationships of a personal nature can be problematic and often through no real fault of your own. Inevitably though suffering brings a better understanding, both of yourself and of the world around you. With a fondness for travel you appreciate beauty and harmony wherever you encounter them and hate disorder and strife.

You are probably very fond of literature and could make a good writer or speaker yourself. The imagination that you possess can be readily translated into creativity and you might come across as an incurable romantic. Being naturally receptive your intuition is strong, in many cases verging on a mediumistic quality that sets you apart from the world. You might not be rich in hard cash terms and yet the gifts that you possess and display, when used properly, are worth more than gold.

THE ASTRAL DIARY

How the diagrams work

Through the *picture diagrams* in the Astral Diary I want to help you to plot your year. With them you can see where the positive and negative aspects will be found each month. To make the most of them all you have to do is remember where and when!

Let me show you how they work . . .

THE MONTH AT A GLANCE

Just as there are twelve separate Zodiac Signs, so Astrologers believe that each sign has twelve separate aspects to life. Each of the twelve segments relates to a different personal aspect. I number and list them all every month as a key so that their meanings are always clear.

The twelve major aspects of your life

Symbols above the box mean 'positive'

Shading inside the box means 'ordinary'

| 1 | 2 | 3 | 4 | 5 | 6 | 7 | 8 | 9 | 10 | 11 | 12 |

Symbol below the box means 'negative'

I have designed this chart to show you how and when these twelve different aspects are being influenced throughout the year. When the number rests comfortably in its shaded box, nothing out of the ordinary is to be expected. However, when a box turns white, then you should expect influences to become active in this area of your life. Where the influence is positive I have raised a smiling sun above its number. Where it is a negative, I hang a little rain cloud beneath it.

YOUR ENERGY RHYTHM CHART

On the opposite page is a picture diagram in which I am linking your zodiac group to the rhythm of the moon. In doing this I have calculated when you will be gaining strength from its influence and equally when you may be weakened by it.

If you think of yourself as being like the tides of the ocean then you may understand how your own energies must rise and fall too. And if you understand how it works and when it is working, then you can better organise your activities to achieve more and get things done more easily.

YOUR ENERGY-RHYTHM CHART

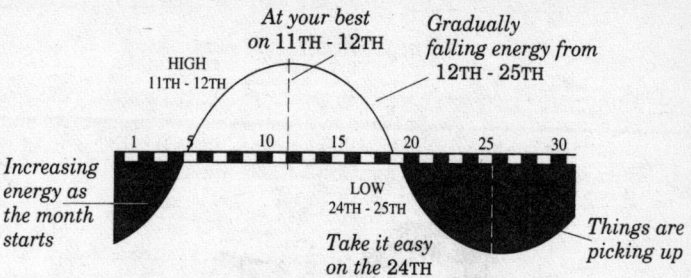

At your best
on 11TH - 12TH

HIGH
11TH - 12TH

Gradually
falling energy from
12TH - 25TH

Increasing
energy as
the month
starts

LOW
24TH - 25TH

Take it easy
on the 24TH

Things are
picking up

MOVING PICTURE SCREEN
Measured every week

LOVE, LUCK, MONEY & VITALITY

I hope that the diagram below offers more than a little fun. It is
very easy to use. The bars move across the scale to give you some
idea of the strength of opportunities open to you in each of the four
areas. If LOVE stands at plus 4, then get out and put yourself
about, because in terms of romance, things should be going your
way. When the bar moves backwards then the opportunities are
weakening and when it enters the negative scale, then romance
should not be at the top of your list.

Love at +4
promises a
romantic
week

ot a good
ek for
oney

← NEGATIVE TREND

POSITIVE TREND →

-5	-4	-3	-2	-1		+1	+2	+3	+4	+5
					LOVE					
					MONEY					
					LUCK					
					VITALITY					

elow
verage
r vitality

And your luck
in general
is good

And Finally:

am ....

pm .... 🔑 ....

The two lines that are left blank in each daily entry of the Astral
Diary are for your own personal use. You may find them ideal for
keeping a check on birthdays or appointments, though it could be an
idea to make notes from the astrological trends and diagrams a few
weeks in advance. Some of the lines carry a key, as above. These
days are important because they indicate the working of
'astrological cycles' in your life. The key readings show how best you
can act, react or simply work within them for greater success.

YOUR MONTH AT A GLANCE

The twelve numbered boxes represent the important areas in your life.
The key to the numbers you will find beneath the panel. A sun above the
number indicates that opportunities are around. A cloud below the
number, that you should be a bit defensive. Nothing above or below and
life will be pretty ordinary.

1	2	3	4	5	6	7	8	9	10	11	12

(sun above 3 and 6; cloud below 5, 10 and 12)

KEY

1 Strength of Personality
2 Personal Finance
3 Useful Information Gathering
4 Domestic Affairs
5 Pleasure & Romance
6 Effective Work & Health

7 One to One Relationships
8 Questioning, Thinking & Deciding
9 External Influences / Education
10 Career Aspirations
11 Teamwork Activities
12 Unconscious Impulses

OCTOBER HIGHS AND LOWS

Here, I show how the rhythm of the Moon will affect you this month. Like
the tide, your energies and abilities will rise and fall with its pattern.
When it is above the date line, go-for-it. When it is below the line you
should be resting.

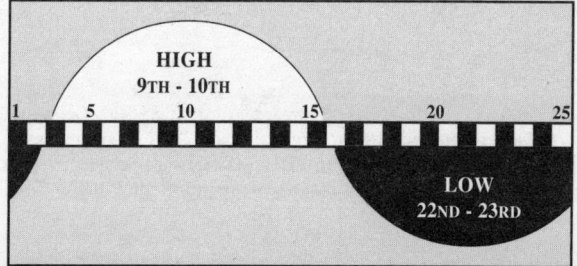

HIGH
9TH - 10TH

LOW
22ND - 23RD

7 MONDAY
Moon Age Day 24 • Moon Sign Leo

am ....

pm ....
A loved one is inclined to feel rather insecure today and will need constant assurance from you if they are not be suffering quite a lot in one way or another. This sort of support is not at all difficult for you to offer when you are in the mood, and you have rarely been more supportive than you are at present.

8 TUESDAY
Moon Age Day 25 • Moon Sign Leo

am ....

pm ....
With a light-hearted and carefree attitude to everyday events, you should see this as an excellent time for leisure, possibly even for celebrations of one sort or another. You are well thought of socially, actively seeking and finding the limelight. Most important of all, you can establish a good balance between pleasure and business.

9 WEDNESDAY
Moon Age Day 26 • Moon Sign Virgo

am ....

pm ....
The Moon returns to your sign, so that energy and enthusiasm in abundance attend your life today. Put your best foot forward and press on with all current plans with the vigour that is so typical of your sign at the moment. Your ability to attract fortunate situations is certainly in operation right now and there are people around begging to help you.

10 THURSDAY
Moon Age Day 27 • Moon Sign Virgo

am ....

pm ....
Thursday shows you pushing forward, indicating that you offer an attractive face to the world at large. Unattached Virgoans should be finding new romantic proposals on offer, possibly associated in some way with work. For all of you the feeling of optimism runs high, though you are unable to go it alone.

11 FRIDAY
Moon Age Day 28 • Moon Sign Virgo

am...

pm...
The emotional peak is followed by one relating to personal popularity.
You might find yourself to be everyone's favourite person at present and
though this could lead to some jealousy or envy coming from the direction
of others, this is generally a time for harmony and enjoying good times.
Your rapport with others is important.

12 SATURDAY
Moon Age Day 0 • Moon Sign Libra

am...

pm...
Despite the arrival of Saturday, this is very much a business as usual
sort of day. Working Taureans can make favourable progress, but even
in this case you should not allow this to prevent you from considering new
plans of a more social nature. Friends, or even your partner may rely
upon you quite heavily and you should be happy to offer support.

13 SUNDAY
Moon Age Day 1 • Moon Sign Libra

am...

pm...
Time spent alone, or perhaps with someone who is very dear to you is
time well spent. Put serious obligations back in the cupboard when it
proves possible to do so and don't be surprised if all practical matters
appear to be a chore just now. Turning down social invitations is
unavoidable, but will not cause problems if your motives are suspect.

← *NEGATIVE TREND*						*POSITIVE TREND* →				
-5	-4	-3	-2	-1		+1	+2	+3	+4	+5
					LOVE					
					MONEY					
					LUCK					
					VITALITY					

14 MONDAY
Moon Age Day 2 • Moon Sign Scorpio

am ....

pm ....
Your mind is almost anywhere but on the task in hand, particularly
regarding work plans or practical matters generally. It is easy to become
bored with the hum-drum reality of life and the secret is to find
something new and pleasant to distract you. Keep such considerations
to the correct time of course and avoid being pushy.

15 TUESDAY
Moon Age Day 3 • Moon Sign Scorpio

am ....

pm ....
You can now find yourself involved much more than usual in a colleague's or friend's emotional problems. The private lives of others
become public as far as you are concerned and your assistance is being
counted on. You can certainly impart some of your age-old wisdom today
and it is well received.

16 WEDNESDAY
Moon Age Day 4 • Moon Sign Sagittarius

am ....

pm ....
There may be unexpected emotional issued to contend with today.
Romance throws up the odd problem, some of which prove to be self-
created. Take the time and trouble necessary to sort them out carefully
and also get your priorities right at work, where there is much at stake.
Continued reliance on others is tedious now.

17 THURSDAY
Moon Age Day 5 • Moon Sign Sagittarius

am ....

pm ....
Some caution is necessary as you are accused today of thinking about
number one. It is possible that such an accusation comes from someone
who is used to having all their own way with you, which is much less
likely just at present. As long as you can justify your own actions to
yourself, there is really no problem.

18 FRIDAY
Moon Age Day 6 • Moon Sign Capricorn

am ....

pm ....
Meetings and appointments may need double checking. With a tendency to overlook necessary details, talks or more casual discussions stimulate your emotions, leading ultimately to strong words on both sides. Where others are concerned, you are inclined to act as a go-between and may just get yourself in social hot water as a result.

19 SATURDAY
Moon Age Day 7 • Moon Sign Capricorn

am ....

pm ....
All social discussions, or important negotiations go smoothly as you are so much in touch with the thoughts and feelings of those close to you. Even usually awkward colleagues can be turned to your advantage with care, and your intuitions will tell you all you need to know about the world around you. Any lack of trust is temporary.

20 SUNDAY
Moon Age Day 8 • Moon Sign Aquarius

am ....

pm ....
Some rather tense aspects cropping up in your solar chart indicate that others are almost certain to point to what they see as flaws within your nature. Since this aspect can also make you more sensitive than might normally be the case, it would be a good idea not to take too much notice of what is being said.

← NEGATIVE TREND						POSITIVE TREND →				
-5	-4	-3	-2	-1		+1	+2	+3	+4	+5
					LOVE					
					MONEY					
					LUCK					
					VITALITY					

21 MONDAY
Moon Age Day 9 • Moon Sign Aquarius

am ....

pm ....
People who are important to you, if only in a professional sense, have
something important to put upon your shoulders. You will really not
want to let anyone down just at present and can work minor miracles if
you choose to set your mind to it. Long-term changes could be looked at
realistically in the next day or two.

22 TUESDAY
Moon Age Day 10 • Moon Sign Aquarius

am ....

pm ....
The lunar low arrives along with Tuesday, making it necessary to put
present schemes on the shelf for the next couple of days. This is an ideal
period to be finishing off routine tasks left over from the past and look
to your partner to come through where your own efforts seem to get you
nowhere.

23 WEDNESDAY
Moon Age Day 11 • Moon Sign Pisces

am ....

pm ....
With the lunar low still around, you are not at your most physically
energetic to meet the working week. Routine tasks will be the best ones
to undertake now, leaving important decision making until later. Setbacks to routines can be aggravating, though not in the long term. Count
on the support of others for a while.

24 THURSDAY
Moon Age Day 12 • Moon Sign Pisces

am ....

pm ....
Divided loyalties now become possible, especially if you allow yourself to
get between loved ones and friends when any sort of dispute is likely.
Perhaps it would be best to avoid any such situation and to do your best
to pour oil on troubled waters if you cannot help being drawn into the
situation somehow.

44

25 FRIDAY
Moon Age Day 13 • Moon Sign Aries

am..

pm..
The most casual social conversations can become heated now, as combined influences at present in your chart, create a more combative Virgoan than would generally be the case. Nevertheless you don't have all the answers and must allow for necessary differences of opinion, but aside from confrontations, the day ought to be eventful.

26 SATURDAY
Moon Age Day 14 • Moon Sign Aries

am..

pm..
Although the weekend is here, don't be surprised if some professional issues get the go-ahead now. In most areas of your life, you are now in a position to affect the course of events. Your personal intuition is high and others are inclined to turn to you for leadership. Those in authority should be impressed.

27 SUNDAY
Moon Age Day 15 • Moon Sign Taurus

am..

pm..
Hunches tend to be worth listening to, and can be acted upon in all cases. There is a side to your mind that other types do not enjoy to the same extent, so you really cannot expect others to rely quite so much on gut reactions as you tend to do. Certain aspects of the past must be faced up to at the present time.

← *NEGATIVE TREND*								*POSITIVE TREND* →			
-5	-4	-3	-2	-1			+1	+2	+3	+4	+5
					LOVE						
					MONEY						
					LUCK						
					VITALITY						

28 MONDAY
Moon Age Day 16 • Moon Sign Taurus

am ....

pm ....
At the start of a new and favourable working week, you can almost instantly make a good impression on colleagues or associates. Good news arrives regarding ambitions and plans of a professional nature. It should also be an advantageous time financially with money resources boosted by an agreeable and compromising atmosphere.

29 TUESDAY
Moon Age Day 17 • Moon Sign Gemini

am ....

pm ....
The best time of all to put new ideas into action, no matter if they are large or small. A colleague or a friend can be relied upon to take your side and help you out in any way that they can. You can also reap some of the benefits from the help and support that you have been so willing to show to others this month.

30 WEDNESDAY
Moon Age Day 18 • Moon Sign Gemini

am ....

pm ....
Not all the help that you require today comes from the directions that you would expect, and so you should get yourself used to the prospects of some surprises before the day is out. A good time to be re-establishing social contacts that have fallen by the wayside recently, and for making new friends at some stage.

31 THURSDAY
Moon Age Day 19 • Moon Sign Cancer

am ....

pm ....
At the end of October you need to toe the line as circumstances conspire to limit your freedom. Avoid planning too far ahead and ensure that your obligations and duties regarding others are attended to before you move on. Taking on too many commitments now would certainly be a mistake and a little rest would be of good.

1 FRIDAY
Moon Age Day 20 • Moon Sign Cancer

am..

pm..
Perhaps you are not quite so sensible at the start of this month as you were earlier, mainly because you do not care for the attitude of those around you. This could be sort of Friday when many Virgoans would be seeking a little solitude, and there is no doubt that you can make gains from being alone.

2 SATURDAY
Moon Age Day 21 • Moon Sign Cancer

am..

pm..
A few problems are turned round cleverly now meaning that rewards come especially from the direction of your house and home during the next week or two. Some slight tendency to be impulsive should be more than countered by an ability to get things done in a constructive manner, both at home and at work.

3 SUNDAY
Moon Age Day 22 • Moon Sign Leo

am..

pm..
You now have the chance to get yourself out of some sort of financial rut and would be well advised to do so. In amongst thoughts about the money aspects of your life you should not lose sight of the personal side of life. In many respects this has rarely been better, though there could be niggles at home.

← *NEGATIVE TREND*   *POSITIVE TREND* →

-5	-4	-3	-2	-1			+1	+2	+3	+4	+5
					LOVE						
					MONEY						
					LUCK						
					VITALITY						

1996

YOUR MONTH AT A GLANCE

The twelve numbered boxes represent the important areas in your life. The key to the numbers you will find beneath the panel. A sun above the number indicates that opportunities are around. A cloud below the number, that you should be a bit defensive. Nothing above or below and life will be pretty ordinary.

1	2	3	4	5	6	7	8	9	10	11	12

KEY

1 Strength of Personality
2 Personal Finance
3 Useful Information Gathering
4 Domestic Affairs
5 Pleasure & Romance
6 Effective Work & Health

7 One to One Relationships
8 Questioning, Thinking & Deciding
9 External Influences / Education
10 Career Aspirations
11 Teamwork Activities
12 Unconscious Impulses

NOVEMBER HIGHS AND LOWS

Here, I show how the rhythm of the Moon will affect you this month. Like the tide, your energies and abilities will rise and fall with its pattern. When it is above the date line, go-for-it. When it is below the line you should be resting.

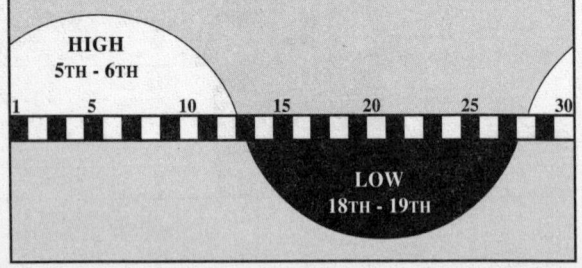

HIGH
5TH - 6TH

LOW
18TH - 19TH

4 MONDAY
Moon Age Day 23 • Moon Sign Leo

am...

pm...
Minor financial gains are possible, and as your mind is working very
quickly at present, you should be in a good position to make the best of
them. Loved-ones may be more than willing to let you know how much
they care about you and of course you will want to show them much
affection in return.

5 TUESDAY
Moon Age Day 24 • Moon Sign Virgo

am...

pm...
An excellent day to get stuck into all those jobs that have been hanging
around for so long. With the lunar high now working for you positively,
you will also want to make the most of new opportunities that come your
way. There is more than a chance that you will find finances strength-
ening significantly.

6 WEDNESDAY
Moon Age Day 25 • Moon Sign Virgo

am...

pm...
Good luck appears to be easier to find, as the week reaches its half way
stage. Almost everyone that you come across seems to be in the right
mood to do you some favours, and you can take advantage of the fact,
without feeling that you are putting on the people concerned.

7 THURSDAY
Moon Age Day 26 • Moon Sign Virgo

am...

pm...
Trying to please everyone at once could again prove to be something of
a problem for you today. The people with whom you live and work could
be expecting far more of you in some ways than you are either willing or
able to give. Important personal plans should be pressed ahead with, no
matter what.

8 FRIDAY
Moon Age Day 27 • Moon Sign Libra

am...

pm...
What a good day this would be for spring-cleaning, even though the Autumn is now well and truly here. You may find that it is the way you think that needs a little organising, but there are people around who can be of significant assistance. A really difficult person may cease to have a place in your life quite soon.

9 SATURDAY
Moon Age Day 28 • Moon Sign Libra

am...

pm...
You can work long and hard this weekend in pursuit of your own idea of success. There are few people about who would have sufficient strength of character to tell you that you are not doing the things that you should be, though if you are perceptive, you could hardly fail to notice their attitudes.

10 SUNDAY
Moon Age Day 29 • Moon Sign Scorpio

am...

pm...
People want to set themselves up to prove that they can do certain things better than you can. In most respects there is no competition and you will have nothing to prove. However you can be very determined on occasions and could easily rise to the bait in some way before the day is finally over.

← *NEGATIVE TREND*   *POSITIVE TREND* →

-5	-4	-3	-2	-1			+1	+2	+3	+4	+5
					LOVE						
					MONEY						
					LUCK						
					VITALITY						

11 MONDAY
Moon Age Day 0 • Moon Sign Scorpio

am ....

pm ....
A high profile day is probably on offer for most Virgo subjects now, and your ability to get on well with others is especially worthy of note. Even so, it is important not to agree with others simply for the sake of doing so. Your own opinion proves to be important to most people in any case.

12 TUESDAY
Moon Age Day 1 • Moon Sign Sagittarius

am ....

pm ....
Life speeds up. Communication becomes easier with present trends predominating. So much so, that colleagues and friends alike will have great difficulty in keeping you quiet. A jokey atmosphere prevails, perpetuated by your present attitude and the involvement of new and interesting people who come on the scene.

13 WEDNESDAY
Moon Age Day 2 • Moon Sign Sagittarius

am ....

pm ....
Others could appear to be moving forward at your expense. However, look around you because later on your partner, or close friends, can prove to be most helpful. Some residual frustration now merely serves as an incentive for future efforts on your part and patience is required today.

14 THURSDAY
Moon Age Day 3 • Moon Sign Sagittarius

am ....

pm ....
Anxious for new experiences, for fresh fields and pastures new; anything old, unusual or curious captivates your imagination now. Your powers of intuition are at a peak and life's natural magic is all around. Use this period wisely because it is not the sort of time that crops up all that often. Coincidences are almost certain to carry a message.

15 FRIDAY
Moon Age Day 4 • Moon Sign Capricorn

am..

pm..
There are generous offers about, many of them pointing in your direction. Financial propositions deserve a second look, though all situations need to be checked carefully before final decisions are made. This is a productive time, when you are likely to have your hands full, both domestically and with regard to the family.

16 SATURDAY
Moon Age Day 5 • Moon Sign Capricorn

am..

pm..
Despite significant confidence and strength of character, when dealing with everyday situations, the competitive quality of your nature tends to be overplayed. Today you can see challenges where there are none, and would be well advised to find positive outlets for excess energy. Important friends have some good ideas.

17 SUNDAY
Moon Age Day 6 • Moon Sign Aquarius

am..

pm..
Take extra care when discussing delicate personal issues, relating to close family members. The more straight forward you are in your approach, though without being blunt, the better. Joint financial plans could be somewhat unsettling and corrective action is required if you are not to create a situation that could be worrying later.

←	NEGATIVE TREND						POSITIVE TREND			→	
-5	-4	-3	-2	-1			+1	+2	+3	+4	+5
					LOVE						
					MONEY						
					LUCK						
					VITALITY						

18 MONDAY
Moon Age Day 7 • Moon Sign Aquarius

am ....

pm ....
At the start of a new working week, it isn't exactly easy to find that the lunar low is causing some lethargy. Hold back with major plans until you recognise that the time is right, because you can achieve much more at the beginning of this week by simply sitting and watching the world go by, and then by acting later.

19 TUESDAY
Moon Age Day 8 • Moon Sign Pisces

am ....

pm ....
Minor hold-ups are still likely, though this does not mean that you should kiss goodbye to any form of progress today. On the contrary, it is below the surface of ordinary life that you can expect to see some real progress being made, and also through relationships, which should be working out well. A time to plan.

20 WEDNESDAY
Moon Age Day 9 • Moon Sign Pisces

am ....

pm ....
Your life partner, or a close friend, can easily bring out the best in you today. Others seem determined to make social plans on your account and for once you are happy to let them have their own way. Life shows a distinct lack of pressure. Take the lead in social arrangements requiring your special touch.

21 THURSDAY
Moon Age Day 10 • Moon Sign Aries

am ....

pm ....
All practical projects will now show a swifter progress than of late. Today's decisions spring from an accurate assessment of situations and lead to more definite actions in the fullness of time. Where setbacks do occur, you should realise that these merely modify your opinions and strengthen your will. Not a time to leave things to others.

22 FRIDAY

Moon Age Day 11 • Moon Sign Aries

am ....

pm ....
You do need to pay more attention to detail and to keep you hand on the
pulse of all of life's activities. This means splitting your time rather
carefully and not being willing to rest on your laurels, even regarding
situations that are turning out well. There should be time to socialise
and to be the centre of attraction later in the day.

23 SATURDAY

Moon Age Day 12 • Moon Sign Taurus

am ....

pm ....
This should be a very good day for shopping for the home, or for any sort
of DIY project, but you can't expect everyone to agree with your point of
view at present. Some selfish attitude are likely at this time, but you
could avoid major upsets of disagreements further down the line.
Certain people rely upon you heavily.

24 SUNDAY

Moon Age Day 13 • Moon Sign Taurus

am ....

pm ....
A physical boost comes along, during which you should feel energetic and
ready for almost anything. Competitiveness is almost certain with
trends being what they are, but don't allow this to get out of hand,
particularly in social situations. There are points to be proved today, but
there is also the tendency to overstep the mark.

← *NEGATIVE TREND*						*POSITIVE TREND* →				
-5	-4	-3	-2	-1		+1	+2	+3	+4	+5
					LOVE					
					MONEY					
					LUCK					
					VITALITY					

25 MONDAY
Moon Age Day 14 • Moon Sign Gemini

am ....

pm ....
All team work and co-operative ventures bring out the best in you at the moment. You will also find that you need to express your caring and sharing side. A close friend could have some inspiring news to impart which puts you in a favourable frame of mind. In professional matters it's business as usual.

26 TUESDAY
Moon Age Day 15 • Moon Sign Gemini

am ....

pm ....
Your own work, plus the obligations you feel towards other people can be something of chore, though the rewards come further down the line as a result of both past and present efforts. Consideration of the plans put forward by colleagues may have to wait until you have more time to think. In the meantime, be tactful and carry on as normal.

27 WEDNESDAY
Moon Age Day 16 • Moon Sign Gemini

am ....

pm ....
Don't let today's actions be dictated by emotional impulses on any level, which is one of the reasons why family discussions may not work out too well now. The other important thing to remember at the moment is that you can't please everyone all of the time and so it may be rather futile to even try. Give and take is important.

28 THURSDAY
Moon Age Day 17 • Moon Sign Cancer

am ....

pm ....
Much of the goodwill that you have shown to others in the past now comes back to you tenfold. Despite your popularity you may be somewhat more ambitious than is really good for you. A hard-headed approach is not advisable at present and harsh words would be out of place. Some small disputes can prove to be tedious but are necessary.

29 FRIDAY
Moon Age Day 18 • Moon Sign Cancer

am..

pm..
Do your very best to get away from routines wherever possible, even
though you want to maintain a business like approach to life. What is
most important is the opportunity to enjoy yourself at some stage,
probably mixing business and pleasure in ways that benefit others as
well as yourself. All matters of friendship are favourably highlighted.

30 SATURDAY
Moon Age Day 19 • Moon Sign Leo

am..

pm..
Self sacrificing or charitable gestures seem to be the order of the day and
are presented with no strings attached. It is possible that others could
misconstrue your actions and so it is very important to explain yourself.
This should not be necessary in the case of close friends or relatives who
are more likely to rely on your judgement without question.

1 SUNDAY
Moon Age Day 20 • Moon Sign Leo

am..

pm..
You could be a little over emotional, so ensure reactions are not out of
proportion to any given situation. Look in the direction of your partner
or a close relative who is able to provide tender loving care and will be
happy to do so in return for similar favours shown by you.

← *NEGATIVE TREND*							*POSITIVE TREND* →				
-5	-4	-3	-2	-1		+1	+2	+3	+4	+5
					LOVE					
					MONEY					
					LUCK					
					VITALITY					

1996

YOUR MONTH AT A GLANCE

The twelve numbered boxes represent the important areas in your life. The key to the numbers you will find beneath the panel. A sun above the number indicates that opportunities are around. A cloud below the number, that you should be a bit defensive. Nothing above or below and life will be pretty ordinary.

1	2	3	4	5	6	7	8	9	10	11	12

KEY

1 Strength of Personality
2 Personal Finance
3 Useful Information Gathering
4 Domestic Affairs
5 Pleasure & Romance
6 Effective Work & Health

7 One to One Relationships
8 Questioning, Thinking & Deciding
9 External Influences / Education
10 Career Aspirations
11 Teamwork Activities
12 Unconscious Impulses

DECEMBER HIGHS AND LOWS

Here, I show how the rhythm of the Moon will affect you this month. Like the tide, your energies and abilities will rise and fall with its pattern. When it is above the date line, go-for-it. When it is below the line you should be resting.

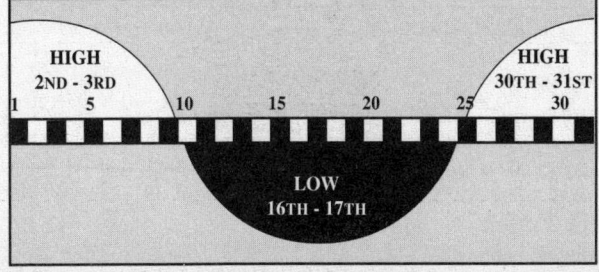

HIGH
2ND - 3RD

HIGH
30TH - 31ST

1   5   10   15   20   25   30

LOW
16TH - 17TH

2 MONDAY
Moon Age Day 21 • Moon Sign Leo

am ....

pm ....
A winning streak comes into your life courtesy of the lunar high and no
matter what situation you find yourself faced with you should be equal
to the task. Any changes to the basic structure of your life can be put into
operation now. The relationships that you form prove to be comfortable.

3 TUESDAY
Moon Age Day 22 • Moon Sign Virgo

am ....

pm ....
Optimism remains high as the Moon remains for today in your sign.
Good things should be coming your way now and there is a possible boost
to your finances, which may not even be related to the effort you are
willing to put in personally. Confidence should be much higher than you
might expect.

4 WEDNESDAY
Moon Age Day 23 • Moon Sign Virgo

am ....

pm ....
Intimate relationships take on an especially warm and sincere feel
today, which could be part of the reason that you are not taking the
practical aspects of life quite as seriously as you will do in a day or two.
Thoughts of Christmas captivate you, even so early in the month, and
forward planning is necessary.

5 THURSDAY
Moon Age Day 24 • Moon Sign Libra

am ....

pm ....
A fairly demanding day, particularly in a financial sense, since there are
certain decisions that you will have to make now that cannot be shared
with anyone else. This does not mean that you find yourself isolated in
a personal sense however, because there is plenty of company available
if you look for it.

6 FRIDAY
Moon Age Day 25 • Moon Sign Libra

am ....

pm ....
There is little doubt that present trends in your solar chart have an enlivening effect on all romantic relationships and though the competitive edge remains in a professional sense, much of your day is spent in high spirits and good humour. A slower and slightly more methodical approach works well.

7 SATURDAY
Moon Age Day 26 • Moon Sign Libra

am ....

pm ....
You now tend to be less in demand than has been the case for the last few days, probably not a bad situation considering that you need time to sit and think. Personal projects feature prominently in your thinking now and though finances ought to be relatively stable, this might not be a bad period for forward planning.

8 SUNDAY
Moon Age Day 27 • Moon Sign Scorpio

am ....

pm ....
Unexpected demands come from the direction of loved ones, perhaps because on a Sunday you are taking more time out to look in this direction. The pace of events begins to speed up, even though the weekend does mean a little more time to do what takes your fancy. Don't be too ready to change your views.

← NEGATIVE TREND							POSITIVE TREND →				
-5	-4	-3	-2	-1			+1	+2	+3	+4	+5
					LOVE						
					MONEY						
					LUCK						
					VITALITY						

9 MONDAY

Moon Age Day 28 • Moon Sign Scorpio

am ....

pm ....

Ever more entertaining company comes your way and you can look forward to a happy time to come, mostly because of the company that surrounds you at the time. Keep a watch out for invitations from both friends and acquaintances, but whilst you are looking ahead ensure that you do not over-commit yourself.

10 TUESDAY

Moon Age Day 0 • Moon Sign Sagittarius

am ....

pm ....

For one reason or another, you may be trying to talk other people into doing things your way and this can prove to be a difficult situation. You may be forced into the position of taking a back seat and of assuming a low profile when it comes to decision making. For now at least, this would not be a bad thing.

11 WEDNESDAY

Moon Age Day 1 • Moon Sign Sagittarius

am ....

pm ....

This is a day for encountering people who are able to contribute to your own feeling of professional success. Present planetary positions increase your communication skills and add to the chance of positive encounters and new friendships. Don't be reluctant to use any situation to your own advantage whenever you can.

12 THURSDAY

Moon Age Day 2 • Moon Sign Capricorn

am ....

pm ....

You show a desire to be friendly to almost anyone you meet and yet much of what you have to say could come across as insincere. Nevertheless, even casual conversations can reveal some surprising and interesting information so it is worth keeping on talking. The hidden aspects of life are important.

13 FRIDAY
Moon Age Day 3 • Moon Sign Capricorn

am..

pm..
Moving away from the rat-race, you are now quite anxious and able to let your hair down. In social gatherings you are the star attraction and the magnetic powers of your Mercurial personality are in evidence. Not a good day for attending to details but ideal for taking an over-view of your life.

14 SATURDAY
Moon Age Day 4 • Moon Sign Aquarius

am..

pm..
The power of your personal influence is strong, though leisure activities may not be quite as exciting as you had expected. Slight quirks in your nature now present show that you are keeping your deeper feelings under lock and key, which could prove to be a mistake if others think you are being deliberately secretive.

15 SUNDAY
Moon Age Day 5 • Moon Sign Aquarius

am..

pm..
Swifter professional progress now becomes possible, even if this is not the case on a more personal level. Relatives come to have a greater need of the unique advice you are qualified to offer, whilst the attitudes of friends takes some thinking about. Social issues start to become very much more exciting.

← NEGATIVE TREND					POSITIVE TREND →				
-5	-4	-3	-2	-1	+1	+2	+3	+4	+5
				LOVE					
				MONEY					
				LUCK					
				VITALITY					

16 MONDAY   *Moon Age Day 6 • Moon Sign Pisces*

am ....

pm ....
Information received in a professional sense makes the path ahead of
you seem much more clear than it has been for a while. This should be
a good start to a positive and fairly busy working week, though it does
demand that you take things steadily for a day or so at least. Plans for
Christmas abound.

17 TUESDAY   *Moon Age Day 7 • Moon Sign Pisces*

am ....

pm ....
A day for putting an end to efforts that have been under construction in
your life for some time. From now on you should have more time to
become involved in the schemes that others are putting forward, and
certainly there would appear to be individuals who are counting on your
assistance.

18 WEDNESDAY   *Moon Age Day 8 • Moon Sign Aries*

am ....

pm ....
Partly as a result of the proximity of Christmas, the most agreeable and
compromising element of your nature is on display. You are also quite
chatty and excel in discussions of any sort. This is a useful time to be
playing go-between where warring parties in the family, or amongst
your friendship circle are concerned.

19 THURSDAY   *Moon Age Day 9 • Moon Sign Aries*

am ....

pm ....
Business and pleasure come together to create one cohesive whole just
in advance of the festivities. Trying to look at only one aspect of life could
be rather counter-productive at present and the best plan of all would be
to go with the flow. Others need to share the limelight, but will you let
them?

20 FRIDAY
Moon Age Day 10 • Moon Sign Taurus

am...

pm...
Good trends attend your life, courtesy of positive alterations in your attitude. In all career or practical matters, help should be forthcoming in furthering your aims and ambitions for the future. If ill-health has been a problem the situation should improve soon, allowing a more energetic approach.

21 SATURDAY
Moon Age Day 11 • Moon Sign Taurus

am...

pm...
At the present time you are somewhat susceptible to negative emotional influences, and need to avoid taking your own moods too seriously. Striking the balance between optimism and pessimism is not easy at present and may not be assisted by the negative attitude of those around you. Stay realistic in your approach.

22 SUNDAY
Moon Age Day 12 • Moon Sign Taurus

am...

pm...
Sunday is productive enough to keep you happy. Many of your efforts are going towards improving the quality of your life, so it isn't really necessary to be busy every moment of the day. Some good luck should be noticeable, especially in a financial sense, though gambling may not be a good idea for the present.

← NEGATIVE TREND						POSITIVE TREND →				
-5	-4	-3	-2	-1		+1	+2	+3	+4	+5
					LOVE					
					MONEY					
					LUCK					
					VITALITY					

23 MONDAY   *Moon Age Day 13 • Moon Sign Gemini*

am..

pm..
Keeping your eye on the ball is difficult and it would be fair if people
accuse you of spreading yourself too thinly at present. Your work, social
life and personal involvements all demand attention, but you will
certainly have to put some issues on the shelf for a while and concentrate
on real priorities.

24 TUESDAY   *Moon Age Day 14 • Moon Sign Gemini*

am..

pm..
There is an element of competition about today, and this is especially
true in the lives of working Virgoans. For all children of Mercury, it is
more likely that you will be persuading people at home to follow your
ideas, though by the evening it is enjoyment that takes over.

25 WEDNESDAY   *Moon Age Day 15 • Moon Sign Cancer*

am..

pm..
You enjoy Christmas Day best this time round if you are surrounded by
a whole host of people. This is not a good time to be on your own too much,
or to dwell on matters that have no real part to play in the day. Coming
to terms with the ideas of others is not difficult and you accommodate
most individuals.

26 THURSDAY   *Moon Age Day 16 • Moon Sign Cancer*

am..

pm..
There could be a powerful psychic link with several people in your
vicinity and this allows you to know instinctively how they are feeling.
Acting according to your intuition would certainly be the best course of
action at present. Boxing Day brings mixed surprises, and the chance to
institute some changes.

27 FRIDAY
Moon Age Day 17 • Moon Sign Cancer

am . . . .

pm . . . .
Now that some of the excitement has died down, it is possible to come to grips with practical and everyday matters, even though some reorganisation may be necessary in or around your home. In other respects this is a fulfilling day, and one that also allows some time to look ahead.

28 SATURDAY
Moon Age Day 18 • Moon Sign Leo

am . . . .

pm . . . .
Able to keep in the midst of good company, you can also be on the receiving end of good news regarding family members and friends alike. Pleasant surprises abound and despite being very busy at home, short journeys and impromptu meetings can also bring benefits. Have a close look at some of your presents.

29 SUNDAY
Moon Age Day 19 • Moon Sign Leo

am . . . .

pm . . . .
A fairly harmonious phase develops, especially in your love life. Sympathetic gestures are apparent in the direction of relatives, and close friends have ways and means of showing you how important you are to them. Don't dismiss your intuition out of hand because it is beginning to work very strongly.

← NEGATIVE TREND							POSITIVE TREND →				
-5	-4	-3	-2	-1			+1	+2	+3	+4	+5
					LOVE						
					MONEY						
					LUCK						
					VITALITY						

30 MONDAY
Moon Age Day 20 • Moon Sign Virgo

am...

pm...
The most rewarding moments today come as a result of the closeness you feel for those people who are most important in your life. It might be a good idea to take a close look at your personal budget and to make some provision for the extra expense that seems to surround you just for the moment.

31 TUESDAY
Moon Age Day 21 • Moon Sign Virgo

am...

pm...
Although you show a tendency now to place emphasis on short term plans for the future, it might be useful to look at the year ahead as a whole. Clear up unfinished business before the end of today and then look forward to the excellent time that is promised, as long as you put the effort in.

1 WEDNESDAY
Moon Age Day 22 • Moon Sign Virgo

am...

pm...
As the New Year dawns you could find that money is uppermost in your mind. There may not be as much to spend as you would wish, and yet most of the greatest pleasures that surround you at this time are not related to cash in any case. Don't allow yourself to be restricted by the negative influences of family members.

2 THURSDAY
Moon Age Day 23 • Moon Sign Libra

am...

pm...
The period of boisterous energy that has been fairly noticeable of late is now coming to an end, which means a quieter sort of Virgoan for a while. You are able to make an equally valid impression on the world however, though tend to do so in a much less hurried sort of way. In many ways a more typical Virgo.

3 FRIDAY

Moon Age Day 24 • Moon Sign Libra

am..

pm..
A steady regime is what you opt for now, and especially so if you are back at work. You can't have everything you want at the moment, though most of the things you need are likely to come your way. Not a time to hang back when it comes to ideas however and you can expect gains later for innovative plans now.

4 SATURDAY

Moon Age Day 25 • Moon Sign Scorpio

am..

pm..
In terms of romance you could surprise yourself now by taking the lead in a new relationship or a new way of dealing with an established one. You should be feeling fairly secure and only too willing to listen to alternative points of view. Restricting influences tend to be left out of any scenario at present.

5 SUNDAY

Moon Age Day 26 • Moon Sign Scorpio

am..

pm..
You are more than able to handle several different tasks at the same time today, but perhaps you should be asking yourself if this is genuinely the right way to behave on a Sunday. It is still very early in the year, so be a little patient with yourself and allow matters to develop slowly.

← *NEGATIVE TREND*						*POSITIVE TREND* →				
-5	-4	-3	-2	-1		+1	+2	+3	+4	+5
					LOVE					
					MONEY					
					LUCK					
					VITALITY					

YOUR MONTH AT A GLANCE

The twelve numbered boxes represent the important areas in your life. The key to the numbers you will find beneath the panel. A sun above the number indicates that opportunities are around. A cloud below the number, that you should be a bit defensive. Nothing above or below and life will be pretty ordinary.

1	2	3	4	5	6	7	8	9	10	11	12

KEY

1 Strength of Personality
2 Personal Finance
3 Useful Information Gathering
4 Domestic Affairs
5 Pleasure & Romance
6 Effective Work & Health

7 One to One Relationships
8 Questioning, Thinking & Deciding
9 External Influences / Education
10 Career Aspirations
11 Teamwork Activities
12 Unconscious Impulses

JANUARY HIGHS AND LOWS

Here, I show how the rhythm of the Moon will affect you this month. Like the tide, your energies and abilities will rise and fall with its pattern. When it is above the date line, go-for-it. When it is below the line you should be resting.

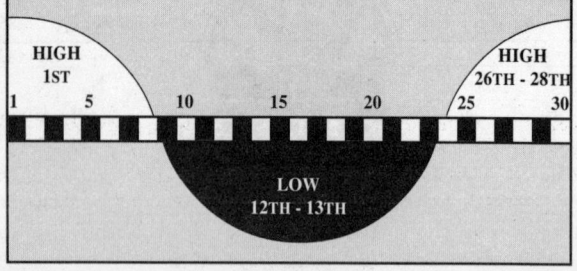

6 MONDAY
Moon Age Day 27 • Moon Sign Sagittarius

am . . . .

pm . . . .

Cultures other than your own might have a part to play in your thinking at the moment and you could learn a lot at the start of this week simply by watching the way those around you are behaving. Confidence may not seem to be an all time high, and yet it is amazing how much you can fool others that it is.

7 TUESDAY
Moon Age Day 28 • Moon Sign Sagittarius

am . . . .

pm . . . .

Favourable circumstances, both at work and with regard to your family life should become evident with today's aspects. Once again it is important to realise that you cannot have everything that you want, though much of what you need should be coming your way. A time to watch, wait and to be very patient.

8 WEDNESDAY
Moon Age Day 0 • Moon Sign Capricorn

am . . . .

pm . . . .

A real red letter day and one during which romance and pleasure take the lead. Although you are probably very busy at work, you do have the ability to find moments to call your own during which you can be sure of making long-term decisions that will stick. The seemingly unimportant now takes on a life of its own.

9 THURSDAY
Moon Age Day 1 • Moon Sign Capricorn

am . . . .

pm . . . .

An excellent time for a stroll down memory lane, and particularly so since you are feeling so nostalgic in any case at the moment. What is more there are gains to be made as a result of taking situations from the past and turning the spotlight they offer onto what is happening around you now.

10 FRIDAY
Moon Age Day 2 • Moon Sign Aquarius

am ....

pm ....
The best of both worlds are available to you now, with work and play both offering tremendous incentives. It is the last day of the working week for many Virgoans, and this is the time when you can lay down your plans for an interesting weekend. Not everyone has your best interests at heart though, so be careful.

11 SATURDAY
Moon Age Day 3 • Moon Sign Aquarius

am ....

pm ....
Whilst you like to keep a centre-stage position at the moment regarding the practical aspects of your life, in some ways you also show a very private side to your nature. Others find this difficult to understand and bringing them round to a realisation that you are not sulking about anything might be difficult.

12 SUNDAY
Moon Age Day 4 • Moon Sign Pisces

am ....

pm ....
Things slow down a little, now that the Moon occupies your opposite sign. The lunar low is not going to cause you any undue problems this time around, though its influence does make you continue the quiet phase which was obvious yesterday. There are splendid possibilities about tomorrow - plan for them now.

← NEGATIVE TREND						POSITIVE TREND →				
-5	-4	-3	-2	-1		+1	+2	+3	+4	+5
					LOVE					
					MONEY					
					LUCK					
					VITALITY					

13 MONDAY
Moon Age Day 5 • Moon Sign Pisces

am ....

pm ....
An unusual sort of day because even though the lunar low is still with you, forward progress looks likely. What proves to be most important is the fact that your any present successes are born out being able to relax and yet find that you are making headway. Probably a hypnotic and quite mystifying sort of time.

14 TUESDAY
Moon Age Day 6 • Moon Sign Aries

am ....

pm ....
You show a much more commanding presence at the moment and can make something definite out of all the thinking that has been going on during the last few days. The attitude problems of those around you are left behind now and there is plenty of support about for the sort of actions that come naturally.

15 WEDNESDAY
Moon Age Day 7 • Moon Sign Aries

am ....

pm ....
Your level of energy is definitely back to the level that you achieved during the pre-Christmas period and you are firing on all cylinders as far as your professional life is concerned. Try not to tackle everything at once today however. It would be quite sensible to leave one or two matters until a little later.

16 THURSDAY
Moon Age Day 8 • Moon Sign Aries

am ....

pm ....
A money or work matter could be of significant importance today and you do need to keep your eye on the ball when it comes to practical matters, concerning which you show a keener than average interest. Take part of today out to do what takes your fancy, rather than having to keep your practical head on.

17 FRIDAY

Moon Age Day 9 • Moon Sign Taurus

am ....

pm ....
With more freedom to chase your own rainbows now, you choose to get
stuck into a few dreams. It does you no harm at all to lay the traces of
everyday life down from time to time and to concentrate on the 'fantasy'
aspects of life a little. Who knows? Sometimes dreams can become hard
and fast realities.

18 SATURDAY

Moon Age Day 10 • Moon Sign Taurus

am ....

pm ....
If certain aspects of life appear to be rather confusing, you can at least
console yourself with the realisation that you have all weekend to sort
them out. Discounting the advice of people who clearly have something
to gain from your confusion, approach all situations with an open mind
and a certainty of your abilities.

19 SUNDAY

Moon Age Day 11 • Moon Sign Gemini

am ....

pm ....
Your powers of attention are better today, not that this fact may prove
to be all that important during the weekend. Still, there are people
around who are willing to listen to what you have to say and who may
be affected positively by your words. Your council is sound now, so
perhaps you should listen too!

← NEGATIVE TREND						POSITIVE TREND →				
-5	-4	-3	-2	-1		+1	+2	+3	+4	+5
					LOVE					
					MONEY					
					LUCK					
					VITALITY					

20 MONDAY
Moon Age Day 12 • Moon Sign Gemini

am ....

pm ....
Professional developments once again become more important, as the
daily round at work begins to take you over again. You are quite willing
to be helpful to anyone, but may not take kindly to being told what to do.
In the main you are your own best guide to life at present and are still
of special use to your friends.

21 TUESDAY
Moon Age Day 13 • Moon Sign Cancer

am ....

pm ....
With the Sun now entering your solar sixth house you can expect a
month long period that brings out the best in all your typically Virgoan
traits. In a methodical but very positive way, you now turn your
attention towards overall success and find that much of spade work has
already been done at an earlier date.

22 WEDNESDAY
Moon Age Day 14 • Moon Sign Cancer

am ....

pm ....
You need to take some time out to do exactly what pleases you.
Remember that you have a tremendous capacity for winding yourself up
tight and that the tension caused does you little or no good. Nothing is
quite as important as it sometimes seems and you are able to worry
about worry itself. Try some meditation.

23 THURSDAY
Moon Age Day 15 • Moon Sign Cancer

am ....

pm ....
Avoid hasty decisions, especially at the start of today. Later on you have
a better sense of your own mind and can be fairly certain that you are
being objective. The timely advice of a good friend would probably not
go amiss, but you need to be certain that the person concerned really does
understand you.

24 FRIDAY
Moon Age Day 16 • Moon Sign Leo

am..

pm..
Expect a warm and affectionate response from others today and that is what you are likely to find. It's amazing how kind people can be and particularly so at the moment. Not everything in life is quite worth the level of effort that you have been putting into it and you should be willing to ease off now.

25 SATURDAY
Moon Age Day 17 • Moon Sign Leo

am..

pm..
With the weekend comes a well earned rest and the chance to look at some matters in a totally new light. Try to keep away from noisy or disruptive types, even though to do so might mean cutting yourself off a little. You can invent you own world now, and can make certain that it is neither loud or aggressive.

26 SUNDAY
Moon Age Day 18 • Moon Sign Virgo

am..

pm..
The best time of all for making a new start or for coming to terms with the way that life is changing in your favour. In advance of a new working week you are peaceful and serene inside, allowing you the most important sort of platform from which to launch yourself into new ventures and original ideas.

← *NEGATIVE TREND*								*POSITIVE TREND* →				
-5	-4	-3	-2	-1				+1	+2	+3	+4	+5
					LOVE							
					MONEY							
					LUCK							
					VITALITY							

27 MONDAY
Moon Age Day 19 • Moon Sign Virgo

am ....

pm ....
The lunar high is still with you, and at this time, whilst the Moon is in your sign, you have much more energy to put into new projects. The start of this working week brings you to a greater realisation of your own potential and also puts you in touch with people who help you with important plans for later in the month.

28 TUESDAY
Moon Age Day 20 • Moon Sign Virgo

am ....

pm ....
A strong sense of purpose that exists around you today shows just how important the lunar high has been for you this month. Now you are taking some of your most important incentives and bending them to suit your present needs. The attitude of friends could be a little confusing at first and you will need patience.

29 WEDNESDAY
Moon Age Day 21 • Moon Sign Libra

am ....

pm ....
Workwise this is a favourable time to put your best foot forward and to back your own hunches, which are very strong at present. A slight retreat from the cares and ambitions of material life would allow you a different view of life and bring you to a better understanding of what you really want to do now.

30 THURSDAY
Moon Age Day 22 • Moon Sign Libra

am ....

pm ....
An excellent time for consolidating your plans and for making them work more exclusively for you. You have shown very few selfish trends so far this year and can now afford to be just a little more single-minded about what you want. In any case, you are able to take others along the road to success with you.

31 FRIDAY
Moon Age Day 23 • Moon Sign Scorpio

am ....

pm ....
If you have managed to overcome a degree of self doubt, there is no
reason why you should not find progress continuing today, though there
are times at the moment when you wonder exactly what sort of horizon
you want to walk towards at all. Dump some of the more tense attitudes
of the past and simply 'be'.

1 SATURDAY
Moon Age Day 24 • Moon Sign Scorpio

am ....

pm ....
A day when things have to be done your own way and when the ideas of
others, no matter how well meant, really do not count for anything at all.
A better set of circumstances personally now seems to surround you,
leaving you feeling a great deal happier with your personal life. Some
magic happenings arise.

2 SUNDAY
Moon Age Day 25 • Moon Sign Sagittarius

am ....

pm ....
Simply being yourself is the key to happiness at the moment, no matter
how you feel about things at the moment. It may not be the sort of
weather to be getting out of doors, though in some ways a little time in
the fresh air would do you the world of good. Stay away from petty
frustrations if you can.

← NEGATIVE TREND							POSITIVE TREND →				
-5	-4	-3	-2	-1			+1	+2	+3	+4	+5
					LOVE						
					MONEY						
					LUCK						
					VITALITY						

FEBRUARY

1997

YOUR MONTH AT A GLANCE

The twelve numbered boxes represent the important areas in your life.
The key to the numbers you will find beneath the panel. A sun above the
number indicates that opportunities are around. A cloud below the
number, that you should be a bit defensive. Nothing above or below and
life will be pretty ordinary.

1	2	3	4	5	6	7	8	9	10	11	12

KEY

1 Strength of Personality	7 One to One Relationships
2 Personal Finance	8 Questioning, Thinking & Deciding
3 Useful Information Gathering	9 External Influences / Education
4 Domestic Affairs	10 Career Aspirations
5 Pleasure & Romance	11 Teamwork Activities
6 Effective Work & Health	12 Unconscious Impulses

FEBRUARY HIGHS AND LOWS

Here, I show how the rhythm of the Moon will affect you this month. Like
the tide, your energies and abilities will rise and fall with its pattern.
When it is above the date line, go-for-it. When it is below the line you
should be resting.

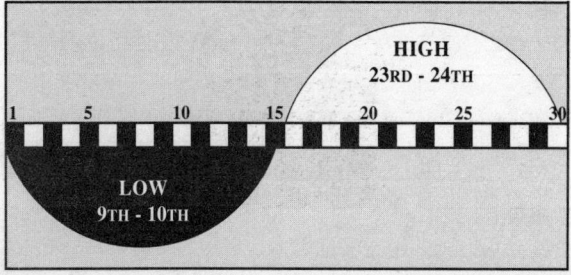

HIGH
23RD - 24TH

LOW
9TH - 10TH

3 MONDAY   *Moon Age Day 26 • Moon Sign Sagittarius*

am...

pm...
It's a 'business as usual' sort of day and not a period for thinking too much
about personal matters. Minor upsets early in the day should pass soon
enough and you will be in the right frame of mind to push forward in new
professional directions. If not an especially happy phase, this should be
a confident one.

4 TUESDAY   *Moon Age Day 27 • Moon Sign Sagittarius*

am...

pm...
There are minor improvements all round, not least of all in a personal
sense. You should be a little happier about the way others are treating
you and will be more willing to put yourself out on their behalf as a result.
A slightly more ingenious Virgoan greets the day and your expectations
are high.

5 WEDNESDAY   *Moon Age Day 28 • Moon Sign Capricorn*

am...

pm...
One thing that you are not likely to do at the moment is to hide your light
under a bushel. On the contrary, you make it plain to everyone you come
across that you are going to do those things that get you most noticed.
The more reserved qualities of your sign are out of the window, at least
for the time being.

6 THURSDAY   *Moon Age Day 29 • Moon Sign Capricorn*

am...

pm...
Your usual love of routine and order shows itself more clearly in the way
that you are living your life today. Everything has to be where it should
be and you won't take kindly to people who wander about aimlessly.
Despite all of this, you know yourself well now and work to the very best
of your ability.

7 FRIDAY

Moon Age Day 0 • Moon Sign Aquarius

am...

pm...
Much effort is now going into the improvement of your personal world
and the way that relationships especially are being dealt with. There is
slightly better luck to be had at the moment, though this is not the time
for betting more than you have. Social efforts on the part of others could
disappoint you.

8 SATURDAY

Moon Age Day 1 • Moon Sign Aquarius

am...

pm...
A slackening of the pace is indicated as the Moon draws back towards
your opposite sign. By the evening you may find yourself to be more tired
than you would have expected, though as long as you realise that this is
no more than a slight hiccup all should be well. Please yourself about
social matters today.

9 SUNDAY

Moon Age Day 2 • Moon Sign Pisces

am...

pm...
While the general trends are somewhat slower you can be certain of
making a more of yourself in terms of relationships. The kindest and
most nurturing qualities within you are now quite clearly on display and
you show the world at large exactly what sort of a person you are.
Finances may not be strong.

← NEGATIVE TREND						POSITIVE TREND →				
-5	-4	-3	-2	-1		+1	+2	+3	+4	+5
					LOVE					
					MONEY					
					LUCK					
					VITALITY					

10 MONDAY
Moon Age Day 3 • Moon Sign Pisces

am..

pm..

After a slow start today offers you the chance to begin building steadily onto a fairly secure fiscal base that you have been establishing since the start of the year. There is no need to rush anything and you should find that opportunities present themselves one after another. Simply pay attention.

11 TUESDAY
Moon Age Day 4 • Moon Sign Aries

am..

pm..

Though you are clearly willing to help almost anyone with anything, you probably should not assume that you have the power to sort everything out yourself. There are times when you have to rely on the support of an expert and this is such a period. Excitement at long-term travel plans can be expected.

12 WEDNESDAY
Moon Age Day 5 • Moon Sign Aries

am..

pm..

Today's planetary aspects make work prospects go with a swing and offer you plenty of chance to put your own ideas into the cauldron of life. While things are bubbling away merrily you will be making the most out of personal and social matters, which look especially good later in the day. Friends assist you now.

13 THURSDAY
Moon Age Day 6 • Moon Sign Taurus

am..

pm..

You are quite prepared to take on more than your fair share of responsibilities today if that is what it takes to get things done. In the main it seems as though others are on your side at the moment and you cannot lose if you are willing to itemise what you are after in life and move steadily towards it.

14 FRIDAY

Moon Age Day 7 • Moon Sign Taurus

am ....

pm ....
If only other people would not interfere with you, then you could get on and make certain that jobs were done in a satisfactory way. Unfortunately they do, and this trend continues for much of the day. All that you can really do is to keep track of the situation and refuse to allow yourself to become annoyed.

15 SATURDAY

Moon Age Day 8 • Moon Sign Gemini

am ....

pm ....
Freedom is still a little constrained thanks to the money matters, which are inclined to press in on you at the moment. Something that you have been putting off needs to be dealt with as soon as possible and you cannot dodge the sort of responsibilities that have been pressing in on you.

16 SUNDAY

Moon Age Day 9 • Moon Sign Gemini

am ....

pm ....
Career matters are looking up, or at least they would be under present trends if it was not for the fact that this is Sunday. The best bet is to plan ahead and to use to the day to your advantage socially. A few timely gestures today can make the future easier to deal with and your time is not being wasted.

← NEGATIVE TREND						POSITIVE TREND →				
-5	-4	-3	-2	-1		+1	+2	+3	+4	+5
					LOVE					
					MONEY					
					LUCK					
					VITALITY					

17 MONDAY

Moon Age Day 10 • Moon Sign Gemini

am ....

pm ....
Now things definitely start to work out as you would wish and you have
no lack of support coming from the direction of friends and colleagues,
most of whom clearly do have your best interests at heart. If not
everything comes together quite the way that you would wish, then you
are simply not looking properly.

18 TUESDAY

Moon Age Day 11 • Moon Sign Cancer

am ....

pm ....
An opportunity exists to make new friends and to influence your own life
to a greater extent than would often be the case. There are time however
when you cannot see the wood for the trees and when you would simply
find it easier to let others make the running. Leave difficult types alone
at all stages today.

19 WEDNESDAY

Moon Age Day 12 • Moon Sign Cancer

am ....

pm ....
It looks as though relationships are working especially well for you at
present and you can make the greatest gains today by being willing to
rely on those around you. Keep an open mind about possible changes in
responsibilities because you can probably find a new way to view
something that has troubled you.

20 THURSDAY

Moon Age Day 13 • Moon Sign Leo

am ....

pm ....
It is time to retreat a little from the rush and stress of everyday life. Of
course not everyone recognises that you need a rest and it is possible that
you may have to let them know in no uncertain terms. Friends do not
conform to your expectations of them at present and some patience on
your part is necessary.

21 FRIDAY
Moon Age Day 14 • Moon Sign Leo

am...

pm..
Your ideas seem to be quite revolutionary to certain other people and
this is a time when it would be very sensible to explain yourself as fully
as you can. Friends are on hand to offer the sort of support that has
clearly been lacking in your life of late and even colleagues come good
before the day ends.

22 SATURDAY
Moon Age Day 15 • Moon Sign Leo

am...

pm..
The Moon moves towards your own sign of Virgo, bringing a time of light
relief and the option to please yourself for the weekend. Using these
favourable trends in a professional manner is once again rather difficult.
All the same you have time to look, listen and plan, and will not be at all
short of energy.

23 SUNDAY
Moon Age Day 16 • Moon Sign Virgo

am...

pm..
A physical and mental peak comes along to brighten up your Sunday no
end. This does not mean that you have to push yourself hard all day,
merely that you can enjoy almost anything that is on offer to the full.
However it also implies that you will start the new working week with
drive, enthusiasm and determination.

← NEGATIVE TREND						POSITIVE TREND →				
-5	-4	-3	-2	-1		+1	+2	+3	+4	+5
					LOVE					
					MONEY					
					LUCK					
					VITALITY					

24 MONDAY
Moon Age Day 17 • Moon Sign Virgo

am ....

pm ....
The green light is on if you have decisions to make and the beginning of
the week should turn out to be useful and entertaining. If you have been
looking for assistance with a new project, than now is the time to cast
your net around and to expect others to come good for you. All in all a
good day.

25 TUESDAY
Moon Age Day 18 • Moon Sign Libra

am ....

pm ....
One of two people are more difficult to deal with at present and you are
going to be in a position which means finding a degree of patience that
Virgo people don't always possess in abundance. The need for freedom
is great at present and there may not be the space to allow yourself the
luxury. Keep a low profile.

26 WEDNESDAY
Moon Age Day 19 • Moon Sign Libra

am ....

pm ....
Other people do not impress you quite as much as you would wish now
and on the whole you tend to spend a little time on your own. This need
to retreat into yourself might not be all that easy to put into practice
during the middle of a busy working week, but you can manage it if you
are willing to divert responsibilities.

27 THURSDAY
Moon Age Day 20 • Moon Sign Libra

am ....

pm ....
Although there may be a slight disappointment regarding a deeply
personal relationship, in other respects the day is good and works very
much to your advantage. There are one or two frustrations to be dealt
with in a family sense too, though these are unlikely to prove serious or
to last for very long.

28 FRIDAY
Moon Age Day 21 • Moon Sign Scorpio

am . . . .

pm . . . .
Things generally are holding together much better than you might have expected, and that means that you have rather more time to give to personal projects at present. The end of the week brings one or two diversions that you certainly have not expected and also means a raise in the level of your personal popularity.

1 SATURDAY
Moon Age Day 22 • Moon Sign Scorpio

am . . . .

pm . . . .
You are doing everything you can to he helpful and to show the kind of support that others see as being so important to their own efforts. Charity matters could be on your mind and you have the ability to help out in a very concrete manner. A few chickens could come home to roost regarding your personal life.

2 SUNDAY
Moon Age Day 23 • Moon Sign Sagittarius

am . . . .

pm . . . .
Your diplomatic skills are certainly to the fore now and that means a peaceful Sunday and one during which you can sow the seeds of later successes. As the day wears on you begin to realise exactly how much is going your way. Stay well away from situations that you can do nothing to improve or influence.

← NEGATIVE TREND						POSITIVE TREND →				
-5	-4	-3	-2	-1		+1	+2	+3	+4	+5
					LOVE					
					MONEY					
					LUCK					
					VITALITY					

1997

YOUR MONTH AT A GLANCE

The twelve numbered boxes represent the important areas in your life. The key to the numbers you will find beneath the panel. A sun above the number indicates that opportunities are around. A cloud below the number, that you should be a bit defensive. Nothing above or below and life will be pretty ordinary.

1	2	3	4	5	6	7	8	9	10	11	12

(Suns above 5 and 6; clouds below 3, 10 and 12)

KEY

1 Strength of Personality
2 Personal Finance
3 Useful Information Gathering
4 Domestic Affairs
5 Pleasure & Romance
6 Effective Work & Health
7 One to One Relationships
8 Questioning, Thinking & Deciding
9 External Influences / Education
10 Career Aspirations
11 Teamwork Activities
12 Unconscious Impulses

MARCH HIGHS AND LOWS

Here, I show how the rhythm of the Moon will affect you this month. Like the tide, your energies and abilities will rise and fall with its pattern. When it is above the date line, go-for-it. When it is below the line you should be resting.

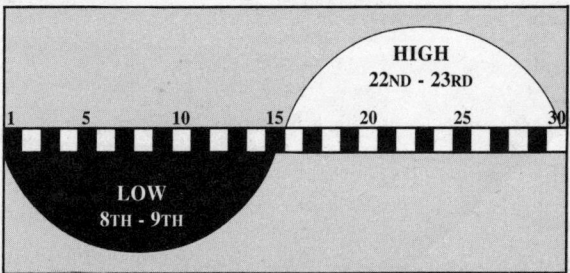

HIGH
22ND - 23RD

LOW
8TH - 9TH

3 MONDAY
Moon Age Day 24 • Moon Sign Sagittarius

am ....

pm ....
It may come as a shock to you at the start of this week to discover that
certain channels of communication are now blocked to you. Any sort of
pretence is a waste of time today as others will almost certainly see right
through you. Take what is on offer today and make the best of it. You
could be surprised.

4 TUESDAY
Moon Age Day 25 • Moon Sign Capricorn

am ....

pm ....
A good period for spending a little more time with family members, most
of whom quite clearly do have your best interest at heart. Relationships
generally seem to be going well and to be offering you the sort of
encouragement that is of special importance to you now. An advantageous time all round.

5 WEDNESDAY
Moon Age Day 26 • Moon Sign Capricorn

am ....

pm ....
For Virgo people who have been looking for love this is clearly an
important time and one that means being able to find the right words to
express the way your emotions are going. Keeping up appearances
generally is quite easy at present and you have the power to influence
the lives of all sorts of people.

6 THURSDAY
Moon Age Day 27 • Moon Sign Aquarius

am ....

pm ....
In a workaday sense this is a time for simply rolling up your sleeves and
for getting stuck in. Not everyone around you seems to have the same
idea and so you are going to have to be especially patient with a few
individuals. There is some frustration if you cannot get on as quickly as
you wish.

7 FRIDAY
Moon Age Day 28 • Moon Sign Aquarius

am ....

pm ....
A colleague or an associate has the same ideas as you and this is a very fortunate time for coming to terms with a new business venture. You may even be joining forces with a relative and making the space you need to create the sort of impression that really counts for a lot. Don't be outdone by anyone.

8 SATURDAY
Moon Age Day 0 • Moon Sign Pisces

am ....

pm ....
Not a time to be driving yourself any harder than you have to. The Moon is not in a fortunate position for you at present and you will find that you are pushing yourself harder than is either necessary or sensible. If you do not have to work today, make the most of spare hours to simply please yourself.

9 SUNDAY
Moon Age Day 1 • Moon Sign Pisces

am ....

pm ....
It may be a wise move to allow others to make some of the running and most of the decisions. You simply cannot be on top form all the time, no matter how frustrating that realisation might be to you at the moment. As long as you do not try to influence too many situations, this should turn out to be a good day.

← *NEGATIVE TREND*						*POSITIVE TREND* →				
-5	-4	-3	-2	-1		+1	+2	+3	+4	+5
					LOVE					
					MONEY					
					LUCK					
					VITALITY					

10 MONDAY
Moon Age Day 2 • Moon Sign Aries

am ....

pm ....
Despite the fact that relationships are going more or less the way that you would wish, you could find that there are a few frustrations still remaining, mainly thanks to the way that other people refuse to listen to your advice. But maybe they think that they have a valid point of view, so do listen.

11 TUESDAY
Moon Age Day 3 • Moon Sign Aries

am ....

pm ....
Don't allow yourself to be overshadowed by anyone. This is the time to be putting your best foot forward and is an opportunity to show the world at large exactly what you are capable of. Your imagination and sometimes your patience is tested to the full, but you always manage to come good in the end.

12 WEDNESDAY
Moon Age Day 4 • Moon Sign Taurus

am ....

pm ....
A period to be expanding your mind and for showing everyone just how capable you are. There are people about who would be only too willing to listen to what you have to say and who have so much regard for your opinions that they will follow your lead. The most important fact at present is to trust yourself.

13 THURSDAY
Moon Age Day 5 • Moon Sign Taurus

am ....

pm ....
Even though your sense of adventure is fired up, you may not have quite the influence to do everything that occurs to you. The truth is that little is beyond your capabilities today, if you only realise the fact. Love comes knocking at the door of your life but only you can decide whether to turn the handle.

14 FRIDAY   *Moon Age Day 6 • Moon Sign Taurus*

am...

pm...
Where joint projects are concerned, it's a case of being willing to listen
to what others have to say. You won't always agree of course, but that
does not mean turning away possibilities before you have looked at them
in a sensible way. Respect and even help comes from some fairly
surprising directions at present.

15 SATURDAY   *Moon Age Day 7 • Moon Sign Gemini*

am...

pm...
Once you have made up your mind to anything today it is very unlikely
that you would change it again. This could cause a problem if other
people see you as refusing to be flexible. In most situations you will be
correct in your judgement, but will still need to exercise a little tact when
proving the point.

16 SUNDAY   *Moon Age Day 8 • Moon Sign Gemini*

am...

pm...
It would be very sensible to take some time out to do whatever takes your
fancy today. You are not going to achieve much by dashing around from
pillar to post on a Sunday and can make greater gains simply by relaxing
and thinking about things a little. Small doubts and fears are not put to
one side.

← NEGATIVE TREND						POSITIVE TREND →				
-5	-4	-3	-2	-1		+1	+2	+3	+4	+5
					LOVE					
					MONEY					
					LUCK					
					VITALITY					

17 MONDAY

Moon Age Day 9 • Moon Sign Cancer

am...

pm...
You may find that other people, perhaps even your partner, may
frustrate one or two of your attempts to get on in life. It is unlikely that
they are behaving in this way deliberately and it may only take a word
or two from you to put matters right. Don't stay quiet though as you need
to speak your mind now.

18 TUESDAY

Moon Age Day 10 • Moon Sign Cancer

am...

pm...
Despite the good things that are happening at every turn, it is possible
that you prefer your own company today and will want to do most things
in your own sweet way. There are small gains to be made financially,
probably simply by being in the right place to see their potential. A friend
may need your special support.

19 WEDNESDAY

Moon Age Day 11 • Moon Sign Leo

am...

pm...
All social and friendship trends look much more secure now and you start
to have a better time out there in the mainstream of life. Romantic
proposals are likely to come good and you start to feel that a long-term
practical objective is going to pay off at last. Not a time to allow negative
feelings to develop.

20 THURSDAY

Moon Age Day 12 • Moon Sign Leo

am...

pm...
You get the impression today that things go better in pairs, and so co-
operative ventures look especially good. This general trend is also the
case in personal relationships, with romance once again likely to play an
important part in your life. You need to think about a communal voyage
of discovery.

21 FRIDAY
Moon Age Day 13 • Moon Sign Leo

am ....

pm ....
Be careful not to let things settle down too much in your life. Today
stands as a bridge between two series of key days and so it might appear
to be rather quiet. However, the Moon is racing into your sign tonight
and the possibilities are endless. Perhaps a few hours rest today would
be no bad thing.

22 SATURDAY
Moon Age Day 14 • Moon Sign Virgo

am ....

pm ....
Your clever and innovative mind is put to the test today and comes up
with all sorts of possibilities that you may not have even contemplated
previously. You feel yourself going from strength to strength personally
speaking and should plan now for some sort of coup that you want to
make at work next week.

23 SUNDAY
Moon Age Day 15 • Moon Sign Virgo

am ....

pm ....
A strong element of luck attends most of your endeavours at present and
you are able to put extra effort into almost every idea that has lain
dormant for a while. If you opt for a small flutter of some sort, make
certain that your intuition is turned up full before you commit yourself
to parting with the cash.

← *NEGATIVE TREND*							*POSITIVE TREND* →			
-5	-4	-3	-2	-1		+1	+2	+3	+4	+5
					LOVE					
					MONEY					
					LUCK					
					VITALITY					

24 MONDAY
Moon Age Day 16 • Moon Sign Libra

am..

pm..
Everything that glistens is not gold and this is a fact of life that could come home to you in a big way today unless you are very careful. If ever you were in a position to be duped by someone, today is the time. Don't sign any papers or commit yourself to any contract unless you are absolutely certain.

25 TUESDAY
Moon Age Day 17 • Moon Sign Libra

am..

pm..
Your competitive instincts are being stirred and you want to get out there and find yourself involved in some sort of contest. It might be an idea to make sure that it is a challenge that you can triumph in though, because you won't like losing at all now.

26 WEDNESDAY
Moon Age Day 18 • Moon Sign Libra

am..

pm..
The greatest gain in life is to triumph over adversity and nobody is better at doing so than you are. If you can take some sort of criticism today and yet still win through in the end, then you are a true Virgoan. Not that anyone who really knows you would ever have doubted the fact in the first place.

27 THURSDAY
Moon Age Day 19 • Moon Sign Scorpio

am..

pm..
There is plenty going on to make you feel fit, active and inspired. This is not the sort of day when anyone would put upon you however, mainly because you would not allow them to do so. If a relative is down in the dumps you are in just the right frame of mind to cheer them up once and for all.

28 FRIDAY
Moon Age Day 20 • Moon Sign Scorpio

am ....

pm ....
Mercury enters your solar eighth house, bringing an excellent period for solving problems of almost any sort. This trend is with you for some days, so this is an ideal time to get the components of your life out and have a good look at them. Relationships that have been sticky now look better.

29 SATURDAY
Moon Age Day 21 • Moon Sign Sagittarius

am ....

pm ....
Be careful that you don't get yourself involved in situations that look fine at first but which lose their appeal very quickly. It might be sensible to avoid any commitment that is not absolutely necessary, at least for now, and to simply get on with the routines of life in your own sweet way.

30 SUNDAY
Moon Age Day 22 • Moon Sign Sagittarius

am ....

pm ....
Try not to get too fixed in your attitudes now, especially regarding a home-based matter. Not everyone is behaving as you might expect and particularly not younger family members. Creating the right atmosphere in which people can be honest may not be easy, but it's worth a try all the same.

← *NEGATIVE TREND*						*POSITIVE TREND* →				
-5	-4	-3	-2	-1		+1	+2	+3	+4	+5
					LOVE					
					MONEY					
					LUCK					
					VITALITY					

31 MONDAY
Moon Age Day 23 • Moon Sign Sagittarius

am ....

pm ....
A much more light-hearted period is likely to get underway today and
you are in the best possible position to make gains from it. It could be
hard to take almost anyone seriously however and this could cause a
slight problem or two if the people concerned are superiors or respected
colleagues. Your charm should win through.

1 TUESDAY
Moon Age Day 24 • Moon Sign Capricorn

am ....

pm ....
Another individual is likely to take on the roll of teacher today, and since
they have something very important to tell you, there is no reason at all
why you should not pin back your ears and listen. Put together with what
you already know, their advice looks like putting you in a commanding
position.

2 WEDNESDAY
Moon Age Day 25 • Moon Sign Capricorn

am ....

pm ....
A more assertive Virgoan greets the day. This is fine, but do make certain
that you do not accidentally upset those around you by making them
believe that you are actually being bossy. A little tact is apt to go a long
way and makes it possible for you to continue to learn from what friends
and colleagues know well.

3 THURSDAY
Moon Age Day 26 • Moon Sign Aquarius

am ....

pm ....
You may have to allow some room for mistakes today, even if these are
not of your own making. Such a state of affairs is unlikely to impress you
but it will do you little or no good to get on your high horse. In any case,
help someone sort out a mess now and they might just do you a
significant favour later.

4 FRIDAY
Moon Age Day 27 • Moon Sign Aquarius

am...

pm...
The Moon is not now in a particularly good position for you, and that probably means that you will be feeling slightly below par. Some concern for a close family member gives you other things to think about and in any case you tend to be rather busy at present. All in all you may not notice the lunar low.

5 SATURDAY
Moon Age Day 28 • Moon Sign Pisces

am...

pm...
Once again you lack quite the drive and incentive that have been so much a part of the last few weeks. Certain matters might look very abstract when seen from your present position, but the truth is that you cannot take a complete view of life at present. Sit back and watch the flowers grow for a few hours!

6 SUNDAY
Moon Age Day 29 • Moon Sign Pisces

am...

pm...
Your ability to think ahead clearly is limited and so you could find yourself with another day that responds best of all to a slow, steady and not too demanding regime. Whatever you finally decide to do with yourself, you would be well advised to take a friend or a family member along. You need some company.

←	NEGATIVE TREND						POSITIVE TREND		→		
-5	-4	-3	-2	-1			+1	+2	+3	+4	+5
					LOVE						
					MONEY						
					LUCK						
					VITALITY						

1997

YOUR MONTH AT A GLANCE

The twelve numbered boxes represent the important areas in your life. The key to the numbers you will find beneath the panel. A sun above the number indicates that opportunities are around. A cloud below the number, that you should be a bit defensive. Nothing above or below and life will be pretty ordinary.

			☀	☀			☀				
1	**2**	**3**	**4**	**5**	**6**	**7**	**8**	**9**	**10**	**11**	**12**
		☁					☁				

KEY

1 Strength of Personality
2 Personal Finance
3 Useful Information Gathering
4 Domestic Affairs
5 Pleasure & Romance
6 Effective Work & Health

7 One to One Relationships
8 Questioning, Thinking & Deciding
9 External Influences / Education
10 Career Aspirations
11 Teamwork Activities
12 Unconscious Impulses

APRIL HIGHS AND LOWS

Here, I show how the rhythm of the Moon will affect you this month. Like the tide, your energies and abilities will rise and fall with its pattern. When it is above the date line, go-for-it. When it is below the line you should be resting.

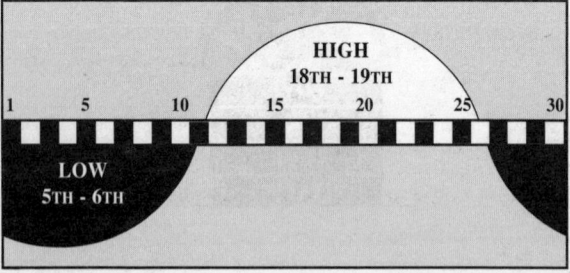

7 MONDAY
Moon Age Day 0 • Moon Sign Aries

am ....

pm ....
The power to turn situations round is now in your grasp and you find
yourself in a good position to take life by the scruff of the neck and make
it do what you would wish. Occasional excursions into worlds that you
are not too familiar with form part of the scenario of today and the
journey does you good.

8 TUESDAY
Moon Age Day 1 • Moon Sign Aries

am ....

pm ....
Your need to be busy and always on the go is definitely intensified at the
moment, and that means that you could easily run yourself ragged.
Certain other people take your capable nature for granted and this is not
a state of affairs that is inclined to help matters much. Try to slow things
down.

9 WEDNESDAY
Moon Age Day 2 • Moon Sign Taurus

am ....

pm ....
Keep as many interesting tasks on the boil as you can today, but try to
avoid taking on too many new ones. The trends of yesterday are still
around and although you may be pacing yourself better now there is still
the chance of fatigue later. Look to the post or the telephone for some
interesting news.

10 THURSDAY
Moon Age Day 3 • Moon Sign Taurus

am ....

pm ....
Insecurity seems to be a fact of life for Virgo subjects at present, though
there is probably not justifiable reason for its presence in your life. It
could be that a little of your realism is going out of the window and that
you are inclined to see shadows where none exist at the moment.

11 FRIDAY

Moon Age Day 4 • Moon Sign Gemini

am..

pm..
If any sort of pressure is on you at work, it is probably to capitalise on situations that you set in motion some time ago. All the same, you can only move at your own pace and would not be inclined to allow force to be applied to your tried and tested methods. Those who try to push you will be disappointed.

12 SATURDAY

Moon Age Day 5 • Moon Sign Gemini

am..

pm..
Despite whatever ups and downs may be evident in your life at the moment, the general direction is onward and upward. However, the weekend has arrived and so if it is possible you need to take some time out to do different things. There are certain to be people on hand who would be more than willing to join in!

13 SUNDAY

Moon Age Day 6 • Moon Sign Cancer

am..

pm..
You will probably be more than willing to watch other people have a good time but could be less than willing to join in yourself. Deep down inside you there is a great deal of planning going on, and most of your schemes will be put into practice in the working week that lies ahead of you. For now, simply sit back.

← NEGATIVE TREND						POSITIVE TREND →				
-5	-4	-3	-2	-1		+1	+2	+3	+4	+5
					LOVE					
					MONEY					
					LUCK					
					VITALITY					

14 MONDAY

Moon Age Day 7 • Moon Sign Cancer

am...

pm...
Whilst you find yourself bursting with enthusiasm, not everything lines itself up in quite the right way today. However, this is certainly not the case in a personal sense, because you have a good time ahead of you in relationships. It is in this direction that you turn once the worries of the day are put aside.

15 TUESDAY

Moon Age Day 8 • Moon Sign Cancer

am...

pm...
Exciting relationship prospects are on the way and they seem to have a much more dynamic feel to them than may have been the case recently. Of course you will have to put yourself out to tell others how you really feel, which is not necessarily easy for a Virgoan. Why not try to write your feelings instead?

16 WEDNESDAY

Moon Age Day 9 • Moon Sign Leo

am...

pm...
Travel matters seem to be uppermost in your mind at this time and even if you are not in a position to be on the move, you may be thinking about planning a journey for later. Speak to someone who has already approached you with an idea for a journey of a lifetime. It might prove to be more than just a dream.

17 THURSDAY

Moon Age Day 10 • Moon Sign Leo

am...

pm...
If it feels as though your get up and go has departed, all that is really happening is that the pressures of everyday life are catching up with you a little. A strain or a sprain is possible if you decide to push yourself harder than you know to be necessary and sporting activities need special care now.

18 FRIDAY
Moon Age Day 11 • Moon Sign Virgo

am . . . .

pm . . . .

What a sudden and unexpected turn round in events. The Moon returns to Virgo and now all the energy you need is at your disposal. Create a special interlude during which you fail to register any sort of impossibility. Everything you heart desires can be yours - well, one or two of your more modest desires!

19 SATURDAY
Moon Age Day 12 • Moon Sign Virgo

am . . . .

pm . . . .

The fact that the lunar high comes along at the weekend means that you are going to be very busy and that there will be little time to stand and stare. Someone who appears to have been rather lacking in enthusiasm now comes round to your way of thinking. The simple fact is that you are so persuasive at present.

20 SUNDAY
Moon Age Day 13 • Moon Sign Virgo

am . . . .

pm . . . .

A sort of transitional period is now at an end as the Sun enters your solar ninth house. You now find yourself seeing clearly towards a horizon that looks far less cluttered than it may have done during the last month. Where you have had to shelve projects, you now find yourself able to push ahead with them.

← *NEGATIVE TREND*							*POSITIVE TREND* →				
-5	-4	-3	-2	-1			+1	+2	+3	+4	+5
					LOVE						
					MONEY						
					LUCK						
					VITALITY						

21 MONDAY
Moon Age Day 14 • Moon Sign Libra

am ....

pm ....
Others will not expect you to be quite as assertive today as you turn out
to be and so you could be shocking them a little as a result. Take any
criticism of your actions and ideas with a large pinch of salt. The real fact
is that there are a few jealous types around at the moment, but they don't
count.

22 TUESDAY
Moon Age Day 15 • Moon Sign Libra

am ....

pm ....
Once again the urge to get out and about is with you and it is likely that
you will feel especially restricted if you cannot get at least an hour or two
away from the same old places. For many Virgoans this would be an ideal
time for an impromptu holiday, or at least for looking again at travel
plans for later.

23 WEDNESDAY
Moon Age Day 16 • Moon Sign Scorpio

am ....

pm ....
A different and quite unique method of getting through your work occurs
to you now and it is something that you can probably put into action quite
quickly. Not everyone is likely to agree with what you have in mind, but
you should be able to bring them round eventually. After all, you are so
very persuasive now.

24 THURSDAY
Moon Age Day 17 • Moon Sign Scorpio

am ....

pm ....
One or two little mishaps could attend your day unless you set out to be
very careful. Nothing of any real seriousness is on the cards but you
could find yourself having to do things again that you thought were out
of the way for good. An excellent time for relationships but not a period
for taking financial risks.

25 FRIDAY
Moon Age Day 18 • Moon Sign Sagittarius

am..

pm..
Something about your domestic life is now less confining than it may
seem to have been. Maybe relatives are offering you the chance to be
yourself and are making fewer demands of you. Whatever the difference,
it is quite marked and allows for a more free and easy attitude on your
part too.

26 SATURDAY
Moon Age Day 19 • Moon Sign Sagittarius

am..

pm..
Some hopeful and aspiring news is likely to find its way to your door now.
It may even be something that you overhear, or perhaps a rumour on the
grapevine. Whatever it turns out to be there is a great deal of sense in
keeping your eyes and ears open today. Others notice a new lightness in
your tread.

27 SUNDAY
Moon Age Day 20 • Moon Sign Sagittarius

am..

pm..
Much of today is geared towards your personal search for enjoyment, so
the practicalities of life could well be out of the window for the time being.
It isn't a bad thing to lay down the traces of responsibility now and again,
and especially not in the case of Virgo, which is often too inclined to work
anyway.

← NEGATIVE TREND						POSITIVE TREND →				
-5	-4	-3	-2	-1		+1	+2	+3	+4	+5
					LOVE					
					MONEY					
					LUCK					
					VITALITY					

28 MONDAY   *Moon Age Day 21 • Moon Sign Capricorn*

am ....

pm ....
At the start of a new working week you are quite keen to strike out on
your own and to do those things that seem to be most important to you.
Some respite yesterday will only have offered you a different perspec-
tive, and this is sure to come in handy this week. A great love of life is
in evidence now.

29 TUESDAY   *Moon Age Day 22 • Moon Sign Capricorn*

am ....

pm ....
You could be feeling especially mellow at present and are more or less
certain to reflect this fact in your association with others. Confirming a
suspicion which has been in your mind for some time should prove to be
possible, though in the main it is the depths of your own innermost self
that concerns you now.

30 WEDNESDAY   *Moon Age Day 23 • Moon Sign Aquarius*

am ....

pm ....
You are ready for almost any sort of challenge, but will not take kindly
to having your ideas scrutinised by people who you do not think have the
necessary knowledge to be critical. Deep inside you find reserves of
contentment and happiness that you do not always recognise. This is a
good time to look at yourself.

1 THURSDAY   *Moon Age Day 24 • Moon Sign Aquarius*

am ....

pm ....
The new and unusual aspects of life demand your attention at present.
Replacing old and worn out values is something that comes as second
nature right now. Give a little time to a friend in need and by the evening
you should be getting involved with new group activities or charity
endeavours that appeal to you.

2 FRIDAY

Moon Age Day 25 • Moon Sign Pisces

am...

pm...

Things are bound to quieten down a little now that the Moon occupies your opposite sign of Pisces. It might seem that your state of mind is a little 'odd' when judged by your usual standards, though you are going through quite an introspective phase in any case. Someone you haven't seen for ages could make a renewed appearance in your life.

3 SATURDAY

Moon Age Day 26 • Moon Sign Pisces

am...

pm...

It is natural to feel quite out of sorts with yourself at the moment, though of course that does not mean that you cannot find something to take your attention and offer a different sort of slant to the day. Someone who is of special importance to you could prove to be all the diversion that you need.

4 SUNDAY

Moon Age Day 27 • Moon Sign Aries

am...

pm...

Although many of your ideas and beliefs may be challenged by others at the moment, you are inclined to keep to the course in life that you have chosen. Sunday should prove to be fairly entertaining but you might find it even better if you spend a portion of it with your family. Confidence is on the increase.

← *NEGATIVE TREND*								*POSITIVE TREND*	→
-5	-4	-3	-2	-1		+1	+2	+3	+4	+5
					LOVE					
					MONEY					
					LUCK					
					VITALITY					

1997

YOUR MONTH AT A GLANCE

The twelve numbered boxes represent the important areas in your life.
The key to the numbers you will find beneath the panel. A sun above the
number indicates that opportunities are around. A cloud below the
number, that you should be a bit defensive. Nothing above or below and
life will be pretty ordinary.

1	2	3	4	5	6	7	8	9	10	11	12

KEY

1 Strength of Personality
2 Personal Finance
3 Useful Information Gathering
4 Domestic Affairs
5 Pleasure & Romance
6 Effective Work & Health

7 One to One Relationships
8 Questioning, Thinking & Deciding
9 External Influences / Education
10 Career Aspirations
11 Teamwork Activities
12 Unconscious Impulses

MAY HIGHS AND LOWS

Here, I show how the rhythm of the Moon will affect you this month. Like
the tide, your energies and abilities will rise and fall with its pattern.
When it is above the date line, go-for-it. When it is below the line you
should be resting.

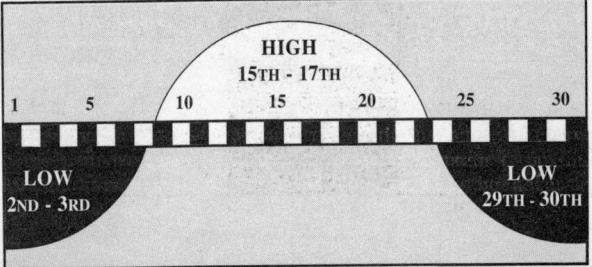

HIGH
15TH - 17TH

1   5   10   15   20   25   30

LOW
2ND - 3RD

LOW
29TH - 30TH

5 MONDAY   *Moon Age Day 28 • Moon Sign Aries*

am...

pm...
Some Virgoans will want to brush up their emotional lives at the moment
and may decide that it is time for a good heart to heart talk. Do
remember though that not everyone is likely to feel exactly the same as
you do and may not be in the mood for a good dose of what you are certain
is the truth.

6 TUESDAY   *Moon Age Day 0 • Moon Sign Taurus*

am...

pm...
Not all the benefits you come across today are going to be exactly
material in type. As long as you are feeling happy you can be fairly sure
that things are going well. As for money, it will be necessary to draw your
horns in a little and simply wait until the situation begins to improve, as
it will soon.

7 WEDNESDAY   *Moon Age Day 1 • Moon Sign Taurus*

am...

pm...
The better weather should be on the way now and you have the same
restless desire that has been with you for some time to get out and enjoy
it. Being stuck in the same place certainly will not hold any real
enthusiasm for you at the moment and it would be fair to suggest that
confinement is out this week.

8 THURSDAY   *Moon Age Day 2 • Moon Sign Gemini*

am...

pm...
You begin to move towards a physical peak now, in fact the truth is that
you probably have a little too much energy for your own good. What you
do with it turns out to be the problem, since not everyone you deal with
is going to want to play squash or go out jogging. Remember that
everyone is built slightly differently.

9 FRIDAY
Moon Age Day 3 • Moon Sign Gemini

am...

pm...
With a strong need to get ahead materially, you may work all hours today in a desperate attempt to get on top of things. All in all this would probably be a complete waste of time when the evidence is that you are doing as much as you can. Allow things to mature in their own good time and avoid interfering.

10 SATURDAY
Moon Age Day 4 • Moon Sign Gemini

am...

pm...
If you are under any sort of illusion at the moment regarding romantic matters, it is only a matter of time before some cheerful soul puts you right. Remember though that everyone has their own opinion and that this does not necessarily mean they are correct. Not a good time to listen to gossip.

11 SUNDAY
Moon Age Day 5 • Moon Sign Cancer

am...

pm...
For those Virgo subjects who work at the weekend, this could turn out to be a fairly positive time in a career sense, if only because others notice just how good you are at getting on with your job. If you do not work at the weekend, you can relax in the bosom of your family, that is if the family will allow it.

← NEGATIVE TREND						POSITIVE TREND →				
-5	-4	-3	-2	-1		+1	+2	+3	+4	+5
					LOVE					
					MONEY					
					LUCK					
					VITALITY					

12 MONDAY

Moon Age Day 6 • Moon Sign Cancer

am...

pm...

A wise old Virgoan greets Sunday, and since those around you recognise the fact, don't be surprised if you are being sought out for special attention. In fact you usually do have a sensible head on, it's merely that people recognise the fact more at present. Wide open spaces appeal to you at the present time.

13 TUESDAY

Moon Age Day 7 • Moon Sign Leo

am...

pm...

You should be able to start the week by ignoring loud, aggressive or difficult sorts, none of whom can be of the slightest use to you right now. Carrying on in your own sweet way, you move towards your objectives slowly and steadily. This may not be your most exciting day, but it does have its good points.

14 WEDNESDAY

Moon Age Day 8 • Moon Sign Leo

am...

pm...

Although you are in one of your most idealistic phases at the moment, you probably should not be all that surprised if the world fails to come up to your expectations of it. Be honest with yourself, but perhaps not too honest for your own good. Your tendency to be self-critical is showing rather more than usual.

15 THURSDAY

Moon Age Day 9 • Moon Sign Virgo

am...

pm...

An increase in your spirits and your physical energy is natural enough when the Moon comes back to your own zodiac sign, though this time round it is also attended by an ability to make positive snap decisions. In fact you are so decisive that you manage to surprise yourself, as well as those around you.

16 FRIDAY
Moon Age Day 10 • Moon Sign Virgo

am...

pm...

A superb time for all new beginnings and for coming to terms with your place in life. Not that a recognition of where you are prevents you from aspiring to be much more. On the contrary you can use today as a springboard into a more successful future. Good luck is with you, though too much gambling is out.

17 SATURDAY
Moon Age Day 11 • Moon Sign Virgo

am...

pm...

The high point continues longer this time around, or at least that is how is might seem to be. The first day of the weekend sees you able to come to terms with jobs around the house and in a position to help close relatives out with projects that are of great importance to them. Most people prove to be helpful.

18 SUNDAY
Moon Age Day 12 • Moon Sign Libra

am...

pm...

Socially speaking this is a time for striking up new friendships and even for coming to terms with people who you may not have had a great deal to do with in the past. It might be sensible to think about securing your future happiness now, but there isn't a great deal that you can do about it now except to plan.

← *NEGATIVE TREND*							*POSITIVE TREND*	→		
-5	-4	-3	-2	-1			+1	+2	+3	+4	+5
					LOVE						
					MONEY						
					LUCK						
					VITALITY						

19 MONDAY

Moon Age Day 13 • Moon Sign Libra

am ....

pm ....
If there is any difficulty covering all your expenses at the moment it might be necessary to hold back a little and to wait until later in the week before you part with any more cash. Energy is not all that great and this is a time that would respond to rather more rest than you have been getting.

20 TUESDAY

Moon Age Day 14 • Moon Sign Scorpio

am ....

pm ....
An important piece of news breaks through the relative gloom of your routines today and should provide a level of interest that has been missing for a day or two. Whether or not you are able to make gains as a result of what you hear may be rather in doubt, but it should jog you into new actions all the same.

21 WEDNESDAY

Moon Age Day 15 • Moon Sign Scorpio

am ....

pm ....
The Sun moves on in your chart into a position from which is has a bearing on the way you see career prospects. For the next few weeks you will be looking at your work through different and more ambitious eyes. Make the most of any alteration that is offered, especially if it brings you more responsibility and more cash.

22 THURSDAY

Moon Age Day 16 • Moon Sign Scorpio

am ....

pm ....
The present position of Mars offers a burst of energy. However, there are so many different directions that you could put it into that it is a little difficult to know where you should start. One job at once would be sensible, otherwise you may run out of steam long before you get anything sorted out properly.

23 FRIDAY
Moon Age Day 17 • Moon Sign Sagittarius

am...

pm...
In your rush to get to the front of the queue in life, you might be forgetting one or two details that are really important. Better to slow things down than to make mistakes that could be difficult to sort out later on. Understanding exactly what others are trying to say will not be easy at present.

24 SATURDAY
Moon Age Day 18 • Moon Sign Sagittarius

am...

pm...
Your sense of your own importance is certainly on the increase, which means you have much more confidence to put in new directions. Interesting projects surround you on all sides, so that is difficult to know exactly what you want to do next. But variety turns out to be the spice of life to Virgo now.

25 SUNDAY
Moon Age Day 19 • Moon Sign Capricorn

am...

pm...
Don't yield too much to pressure at present and do whatever you can to make certain that you are being your usual meticulous self. You won't want to take over the jobs that other people are doing, unless it seems to you that they are not being dealt with properly. A somewhat confusing day, but not unhappy.

←	*NEGATIVE TREND*					*POSITIVE TREND*				→
-5	-4	-3	-2	-1		+1	+2	+3	+4	+5
					LOVE					
					MONEY					
					LUCK					
					VITALITY					

26 MONDAY

Moon Age Day 20 • Moon Sign Capricorn

am..

pm..
You could carry an unusual degree of arrogance around with you today,
so that if the fact is pointed out to you by others, you probably should not
be all that surprised. Delays of one sort or another are not all that
surprising and you simply have to come to terms with them if they are
not to hold you back.

27 TUESDAY

Moon Age Day 21 • Moon Sign Aquarius

am..

pm..
The planetary positions on your chart that deal with career changes now
come to a state during which any major alteration should be undertaken.
If you have made an appointment to see someone who has real influence,
it would be best to go ahead with it. You might even surprise yourself
with your eloquence.

28 WEDNESDAY

Moon Age Day 22 • Moon Sign Aquarius

am..

pm..
Typical Virgo traits are stimulated today, so don't be at all surprised if
your find yourself to be careful, easy to talk to, but probably rather
stubborn too. Not everyone can come to terms with the way that your
mind is working though it is only a matter of time before you persuade
them - or wear them down!

29 THURSDAY

Moon Age Day 23 • Moon Sign Pisces

am..

pm..
Whilst on the one hand you really want to push forward in life, you don't
have all that much energy at present and are responding to the present
position of the Moon in your opposite sign. Regulations are not easy to
come to terms with and there are certain to be frustrations about that
you cannot alter.

30 FRIDAY
Moon Age Day 24 • Moon Sign Pisces

am..

pm..
Today is best served by keeping a low profile and by staying within your capabilities. There is a great deal of happiness around you at the moment and it does not really matter whether or not you are creating it personally. Play down the significance of the way your family are behaving. It probably does not matter.

31 SATURDAY
Moon Age Day 25 • Moon Sign Aries

am..

pm..
Others are more emotionally dependant on you than you might wish them to be at present, not a situation that you are all that happy about. Things may not be going entirely your way at the start of this weekend, though it is only a matter of time before things begin to clear themselves and you gain more confidence.

1 SUNDAY
Moon Age Day 26 • Moon Sign Aries

am..

pm..
You finish the week by feeling rather more cheerful and a great deal more confident. The impact of present happenings within your family now start to have a strong bearing on your own life. Things are still slow, but you can at least be fairly certain that the new working week will start with a flourish.

← NEGATIVE TREND						POSITIVE TREND →				
-5	-4	-3	-2	-1		+1	+2	+3	+4	+5
					LOVE					
					MONEY					
					LUCK					
					VITALITY					

1997

YOUR MONTH AT A GLANCE

The twelve numbered boxes represent the important areas in your life. The key to the numbers you will find beneath the panel. A sun above the number indicates that opportunities are around. A cloud below the number, that you should be a bit defensive. Nothing above or below and life will be pretty ordinary.

| 1 | 2 | 3 | 4 | 5 | 6 | 7 | 8 | 9 | 10 | 11 | 12 |

KEY

1 Strength of Personality
2 Personal Finance
3 Useful Information Gathering
4 Domestic Affairs
5 Pleasure & Romance
6 Effective Work & Health
7 One to One Relationships
8 Questioning, Thinking & Deciding
9 External Influences / Education
10 Career Aspirations
11 Teamwork Activities
12 Unconscious Impulses

JUNE HIGHS AND LOWS

Here, I show how the rhythm of the Moon will affect you this month. Like the tide, your energies and abilities will rise and fall with its pattern. When it is above the date line, go-for-it. When it is below the line you should be resting.

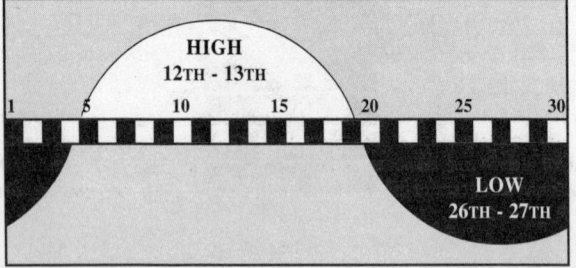

HIGH
12TH - 13TH

LOW
26TH - 27TH

2 MONDAY
Moon Age Day 27 • Moon Sign Aries

am ....

pm ....
There should be every opportunity for a change of scene at the start of this week and you will be snapping up all possibilities with what amounts to a social greed. Your thirst for life knows no bounds and you probably feel that there is plenty to keep you both settled and happy with your lot in life generally.

3 TUESDAY
Moon Age Day 28 • Moon Sign Taurus

am ....

pm ....
There could be a slight mishap regarding professional issues and if so you will just have to deal with the situation as and when it arises. New successes are possible all the same and you push forward when other people would be retreating. Friends will understand the way that you are feeling and want to help you.

4 WEDNESDAY
Moon Age Day 0 • Moon Sign Taurus

am ....

pm ....
The influence of the planet Venus in your chart at present makes for a wonderful period potentially when it comes to social encounters of almost any sort. Of course this depends partly on you too, because if you do not allow yourself to be put in the position of new meetings, the full benefits cannot accrue.

5 THURSDAY
Moon Age Day 1 • Moon Sign Gemini

am ....

pm ....
You are pushing forward very strongly on all fronts, have plenty of energy and a desire to do things that have been out of the question previously. Be certain that you are right in your assumptions before you really push forward however, because there is a chance that hesitation on the way would be a great mistake.

6 FRIDAY
Moon Age Day 2 • Moon Sign Gemini

am ....

pm ....
So much appears to be done in a hurry today that if you are not careful you could find that you do little properly. It is important to pull yourself up now and again and to take stock of what is happening around you. At least this way you don't arrive at the evening rather punch drunk about what the day has been.

7 SATURDAY
Moon Age Day 3 • Moon Sign Cancer

am ....

pm ....
You should be in a generally commanding position this weekend and are certainly going to be calling the shots. In a social sense you may be entering a world that you are not all that familiar with and can gain a great deal intellectually from the experience. A clash of wills could be a possibility.

8 SUNDAY
Moon Age Day 4 • Moon Sign Cancer

am ....

pm ....
Socially you are much in demand, which is no bad trend for a Sunday. Try to stay as close to other people as you can and don't allow a slightly aloof streak to take you over. Even apparently small and insignificant events can have a great bearing on your life in the longer-term, so pay attention.

← NEGATIVE TREND						POSITIVE TREND →				
-5	-4	-3	-2	-1		+1	+2	+3	+4	+5
					LOVE					
					MONEY					
					LUCK					
					VITALITY					

9 MONDAY   *Moon Age Day 5 • Moon Sign Leo*

am ....

pm ....
Others do their best to put you in the know and you might be rather
surprised to discover just how many friends you actually do have at the
moment. Stick to what you know at work, and apply yourself uniformly
to whatever task you have taken on. This may not be an especially
exciting day but it is very useful.

10 TUESDAY   *Moon Age Day 6 • Moon Sign Leo*

am ....

pm ....
After a spell that may have seemed to be rather hectic comes a much
quieter and more reflective period. This is no bad thing for a Virgoan and
means that you have the time to spend thinking about yourself and your
life in general. The only fact that you may not be keen on is a degree of
inevitable boredom.

11 WEDNESDAY   *Moon Age Day 7 • Moon Sign Leo*

am ....

pm ....
By the end of today you might wonder how you ever felt that life was
becoming tedious. It is the way of Virgo to move steadily onward and yet
to discover that life has a different way of making possibilities available.
Excitement becomes the routine now, which isn't especially comfortable,
but is useful.

12 THURSDAY   *Moon Age Day 8 • Moon Sign Virgo*

am ....

pm ....
The Moon is now firmly in Virgo and you discover that almost anything
becomes possible, if only you play situations through from beginning to
end. In any situation your own opinion is likely to differ from those of
the people surrounding you. This does not mean that you are wrong
however, as you will discover.

13 FRIDAY
Moon Age Day 9 • Moon Sign Virgo

am..

pm..
This is an eventful day and a good end to the working week. Once again
remember that not everyone is going to like or believe you. If there is a
problem here it lies in the fact that you have a good sense of your own
abilities, but probably not always the confidence to prove the fact. Much
interests you now.

14 SATURDAY
Moon Age Day 10 • Moon Sign Libra

am..

pm..
Try to make certain that you arrange something different for today. It
would be all too easy to consider that your life was starting to slow down,
and this might come as something of a shock to your system. The truth
is that interest comes from friendship and from the ability to get out and
about.

15 SUNDAY
Moon Age Day 11 • Moon Sign Libra

am..

pm..
There are good potentials for monetary gains today and some of them
come from the least expected directions. There is plenty going for you
generally and you should be in the right place at the right time on more
occasions than not. Don't hold back when you know that you have an
idea.

← NEGATIVE TREND						POSITIVE TREND →				
-5	-4	-3	-2	-1		+1	+2	+3	+4	+5
					LOVE					
					MONEY					
					LUCK					
					VITALITY					

16 MONDAY   *Moon Age Day 12 • Moon Sign Libra*

am ....

pm ....
beware of spreading yourself more thinly than you should. There is good
reason to believe that other people will be trying to confuse you today,
which is not the best state of affairs that you can expect. Work on slowly
and steadily towards your objectives and you cannot go far wrong. Not
an exciting start to the week.

17 TUESDAY   *Moon Age Day 13 • Moon Sign Scorpio*

am ....

pm ....
Put your inventive mind to good use today and don't allow yourself to be
held back by the sort of small difficulties that may have attended
yesterday. Routines are dealt with easily and you find yourself in a
position to make gains from the efforts of other people. Confidences
should be carefully kept.

18 WEDNESDAY   *Moon Age Day 14 • Moon Sign Scorpio*

am ....

pm ....
When it comes to getting ahead generally, this is a time when you will
be using your intuition to the full. Acting on impulse therefore may seem
to be a good thing, though in reality you are being more careful than you
think. Gains financially speaking are on the cards, though may show up
later.

19 THURSDAY   *Moon Age Day 15 • Moon Sign Sagittarius*

am ....

pm ....
Avoid being too heavy handed in your communications with other
people. There are some gains to be made today by being tactful and by
not allowing the more caustic side of your Virgoan nature to show. You
will be surprised at how willing others are to help you out at times of high
activity.

20 FRIDAY   *Moon Age Day 16 • Moon Sign Sagittarius*

am...

pm...
You are much more likely now to play your cards very closely to your
chest indeed. This means that others have great difficulty in coming to
terms with what you are actually thinking. If they have to guess how you
are likely to behave, all sorts of mistakes could be the result. Try to be
more explicit.

21 SATURDAY   *Moon Age Day 17 • Moon Sign Capricorn*

am...

pm...
The emphasis shifts from getting ahead in a personal sense to thoughts
of what you can do for other people. Not everything has been going your
way personally and yet the moment you start putting yourself out on
behalf of your friends you will probably be very surprised at how much
they are willing to do in return.

22 SUNDAY   *Moon Age Day 18 • Moon Sign Capricorn*

am...

pm...
A time to keep trying and for putting in the sort of effort that cannot fail
as long as you keep it up. Relating to those who are close to you becomes
even easier and you should find even more reason to be kind to those who
mean the most to you. Resolve an argument in the family as soon as you
can.

← *NEGATIVE TREND*								*POSITIVE TREND* →			
-5	-4	-3	-2	-1			+1	+2	+3	+4	+5
					LOVE						
					MONEY						
					LUCK						
					VITALITY						

23 MONDAY   *Moon Age Day 19 • Moon Sign Aquarius*

am..

pm..
The help and advice that is on offer today should dwarf anything you
have seen previously this month. Take advantage of any good weather
by getting out into the sun. Even if the storm clouds are brewing this is
a good time to find change and to avoid staying continually in the same
place.

24 TUESDAY   *Moon Age Day 20 • Moon Sign Aquarius*

am..

pm..
When things are not going your way you simply have to be patient.
However, Venus is in a strong position for you and allows romantic
attachments to take on a potentially positive feel at some stage today. A
few kind words now can work wonders in the fullness to time and creates
concrete gains eventually.

25 WEDNESDAY   *Moon Age Day 21 • Moon Sign Aquarius*

am..

pm..
Things are bound to slow down now that the Moon is in your opposite
sign. As a result this is certainly not the best time for putting plans into
action. What you need is a rest and the chance to think certain situations
out in a new and perhaps even revolutionary way. Others find credible
excuses for themselves.

26 THURSDAY   *Moon Age Day 22 • Moon Sign Pisces*

am..

pm..
Your main priority today should be sorting out unfinished business and
doing what you can to get your life onto an even keel. Nobody is better
at this than you are and you apply yourself positively to the task in hand.
Some special event tonight tends to offer more than you might have
expected.

27 FRIDAY
Moon Age Day 23 • Moon Sign Pisces

am...

pm...
Attacking the same old situation in exactly the way you have done in the
past probably will not help you all that much at present. Give and take
are important, especially in relationships and you could find that not
everyone is behaving in quite the way you might have come to expect.
Take your time.

28 SATURDAY
Moon Age Day 24 • Moon Sign Aries

am...

pm...
A day for getting together with friends and for all sorts of discussions,
some of which could prove to be very important in the long-term. Not
everything of significance sounds as if it is early in the day, which is why
it really does pay to keep your ears open, no matter how trivial things
sound at first.

29 SUNDAY
Moon Age Day 25 • Moon Sign Aries

am...

pm...
Your spirits are high now, partly thanks to social meetings and events
of one sort or another, most of which are going your way. The accent is
upon your social life and all that you can do to make it more interesting
and less demanding. Some moments for reflection would seem to be in
order, especially later.

← *NEGATIVE TREND*						*POSITIVE TREND* →				
-5	-4	-3	-2	-1		+1	+2	+3	+4	+5
					LOVE					
					MONEY					
					LUCK					
					VITALITY					

30 MONDAY
Moon Age Day 26 • Moon Sign Taurus

am ....

pm ....
Whoever it is that makes such a powerful impression on you at present, you will want to do all you can to back them up in almost anything they have to say. A slight problem however is that you may not be as realistic as you could be and find yourself easily fooled.

1 TUESDAY
Moon Age Day 27 • Moon Sign Taurus

am ....

pm ....
Don't change your mind over important issues once you have decided on a particular course of action. A reasonable approach is called for in your dealings with the world at large, even if this is difficult to achieve in the case of particularly awkward sorts. A much better day than expected.

2 WEDNESDAY
Moon Age Day 28 • Moon Sign Gemini

am ....

pm ....
You take the world by the scruff of the neck today and can make it do more or less what you want. If you have recently made a commitment to a new relationship, you will be doing all that you can to make things work out well. Where important discussions are concerned, you should rehearse what you want to say first.

3 THURSDAY
Moon Age Day 29 • Moon Sign Gemini

am ....

pm ....
It cannot be denied that you are likely to manipulate others today, though not in a way that should work to their disadvantage. If you do have to look out for the well-being of family members especially, do remember that they have their own point of view too and that, to them at least, it is valid.

4 FRIDAY
Moon Age Day 0 • Moon Sign Cancer

am...

pm...
There should be great potential for making new friends today, something that you will be especially keen to do at almost any stage. A surprise invitation is possible, and this is an eventuality that you should not dismiss, particularly since you can gain a great deal from all sorts of social contacts.

5 SATURDAY
Moon Age Day 1 • Moon Sign Cancer

am...

pm...
Unexpected social calls come your way, and there are reasons why, once again, it is difficult to fulfil the responsibilities that you know you have towards others. Enlightening and informative talks are the order of the day, some of them with people who you find to be especially exciting and able to stimulate you.

6 SUNDAY
Moon Age Day 2 • Moon Sign Cancer

am...

pm...
Changes of one sort or another in your life are now inevitable, though many of these could seem to be rather frightening or at least unsettling at first. The purpose of this key day is that it inspires you to take control of situations, turning them to your advantage and refusing to be manipulated in the days ahead.

← NEGATIVE TREND						POSITIVE TREND →				
-5	-4	-3	-2	-1		+1	+2	+3	+4	+5
					LOVE					
					MONEY					
					LUCK					
					VITALITY					

YOUR MONTH AT A GLANCE

The twelve numbered boxes represent the important areas in your life.
The key to the numbers you will find beneath the panel. A sun above the
number indicates that opportunities are around. A cloud below the
number, that you should be a bit defensive. Nothing above or below and
life will be pretty ordinary.

1	2	3	4	5	6	7	8	9	10	11	12

JULY HIGHS AND LOWS

Here, I show how the rhythm of the Moon will affect you this month. Like
the tide, your energies and abilities will rise and fall with its pattern.
When it is above the date line, go-for-it. When it is below the line you
should be resting.

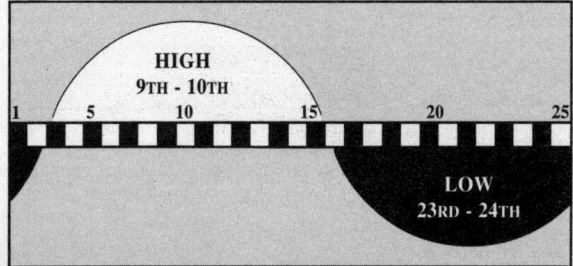

7 MONDAY
Moon Age Day 3 • Moon Sign Leo

am..

pm..
The start of this new working week stimulates the more adventurous side your nature and puts you in the mood to do all sorts of things that might seem to have personal appeal for you. People are reasonable in their attitudes and there should be no end of help on the way for those who are willing to look.

8 TUESDAY
Moon Age Day 4 • Moon Sign Leo

am..

pm..
This is the best period to get plans underway and for making in-roads into jobs that have been waiting around for some time. Lady Luck is on your side and you can take advantage of the fact, simply by being in the right place at the right time, something that comes almost as second nature for the remainder of the week.

9 WEDNESDAY
Moon Age Day 5 • Moon Sign Virgo

am..

pm..
Look around yourself today for the sort of help and assistance that comes from people who are genuinely in the know. This is especially important at work, where you should find that superiors and those in authority are more willing than ever to help you out of any sort of difficulty that comes along.

10 THURSDAY
Moon Age Day 6 • Moon Sign Virgo

am..

pm..
Whatever else you do today it is important to remain as practical as you can, and to keep an open mind about the future. Relationships are on your mind at present and you will probably be doing all that you can to strengthen both family and friendship ties. You might be feeling a little more independent.

11 FRIDAY
Moon Age Day 7 • Moon Sign Virgo

am..

pm..
There is a possibility that you are feeling more romantic today and as a result will want to tell those closest to you how you really feel about them. Confusion at home is not likely to be created by you, and in fact there is a tendency for the people you are closest to turn to you for advice and practical help.

12 SATURDAY
Moon Age Day 8 • Moon Sign Libra

am..

pm....[...
There is great disorder around you at the moment, though it is not actually you who creates it. All the same, there is some expectation that you will sort matters out and that you should take on board problems that rightfully belong to others. In most personal situations, actions speak louder than words now.

13 SUNDAY
Moon Age Day 9 • Moon Sign Libra

am..

pm..
You set out to make a favourable impression on the whole world today, and in the main that is what you are able to do. The secret of success is never far from you, even though it might appear to be somewhat obscure from time to time. Personal developments are positively highlighted at this time.

← NEGATIVE TREND						POSITIVE TREND →				
-5	-4	-3	-2	-1		+1	+2	+3	+4	+5
					LOVE					
					MONEY					
					LUCK					
					VITALITY					

14 MONDAY   *Moon Age Day 10 • Moon Sign Scorpio*

am...

pm...
A high-activity period stands before you now, allowing you to put all
manner of ideas into practice that have been kept to the back of your
mind for quite some time. Confusion can follow for friends, but for a few
days you are in the right mood to sort things out for them. The world
seems to be on your side.

15 TUESDAY   *Moon Age Day 11 • Moon Sign Scorpio*

am...

pm...
Don't let your present need to be the centre of attraction get in the way
of your more practical side, which can be of great use to you now. Loved
ones may not share the enthusiasm which is so much a part of your way
of thinking at present. Stay away from anyone who tends to look at life
in a negative way.

16 WEDNESDAY   *Moon Age Day 12 • Moon Sign Scorpio*

am...

pm...
Differences of opinion arise, and though some of them have nothing to
do with you personally, you would be very lucky to avoid their ultimate
implications. Where you do find yourself drawn into disputes of any sort,
make certain that you know the ground you are standing on to be solid
and truly understood.

17 THURSDAY   *Moon Age Day 13 • Moon Sign Sagittarius*

am...

pm...
There could be some news about that casts a doubt on your personal life,
and you need to take anything that is being said with more than a small
grain of salt. What you probably need more and more at the moment is
a long rest, the only trouble being that there is probably too much to do
to take the time.

18 FRIDAY
Moon Age Day 14 • Moon Sign Sagittarius

am ....

pm ....
Your happiest and most rewarding experiences are those associated with friends and family at the end of this working week. It could be rather awkward to keep your eye on the ball as far as professional matters are concerned and you might be casting your mind forward. A well deserved and well used key day.

19 SATURDAY
Moon Age Day 15 • Moon Sign Capricorn

am ....

pm ....
The social and romantic aspects of your life tend to improve noticeably at some stage today, leaving you feeling very much in command and happy with what life has to offer you in a personal sense. Routine events have a very small part to play in your day, so make the best of change and diversity at all levels.

20 SUNDAY
Moon Age Day 16 • Moon Sign Capricorn

am ....

pm ....
The start of a red letter period with the sun strong in your chart. All incentives to get ahead in a materialistic sense are improved and even though you may not be able to do anything especially tangible about advancement today, the plans are being laid down and your resourceful mind is put into gear.

← NEGATIVE TREND						POSITIVE TREND →				
-5	-4	-3	-2	-1		+1	+2	+3	+4	+5
					LOVE					
					MONEY					
					LUCK					
					VITALITY					

21 MONDAY
Moon Age Day 17 • Moon Sign Aquarius

am ....

pm ....
Although you could find yourself faced with one or two tricky situations at the moment, you come through them all smiling and cheerful. You have everything you need to make life turn in the directions that seem appropriate and should have little trouble persuading others that your point of view is reasonable.

22 TUESDAY
Moon Age Day 18 • Moon Sign Aquarius

am ....

pm ....
Your social life gets a real boost as people gather round to show how much your presence means to them. There is no shortage of attention coming your way from any direction and you have the ability to turn heads wherever you go. A more active Virgoan knows exactly the right way to go about getting things done.

23 WEDNESDAY
Moon Age Day 19 • Moon Sign Pisces

am ....

pm ....
You are able to right certain wrongs, mainly in the sphere of relationships, which are taking a turn for the better now. Creating a favourable impressions is something you know how to do and you keep up a very hectic pace generally. Pace yourself at work because there is much to do and little time to do it.

24 THURSDAY
Moon Age Day 20 • Moon Sign Pisces

am ....

pm ....
You do tend to be a little too self sacrificing for your own good today, probably because of the pressure that you have placed upon yourself in the last couple of days. Don't dwell on the past too much because this tendency will not do you much good in the long run. Certainly a time to look ahead.

25 FRIDAY
Moon Age Day 21 • Moon Sign Aries

am...

pm...
There is plenty of stimuli for new social contacts, even if you are not
exactly in the mood to make the most of them. Much of your life at
present is motivated by the thought of what you can do for others rather
than by considerations relating to yourself. The attitudes of a personal
friend might puzzle you a little.

26 SATURDAY
Moon Age Day 22 • Moon Sign Aries

am...

pm...
You benefit from a really high profile when it comes to the way that you
are mixing with others just at the present time. New friendships could
well come into your life at this time and you are looking at old ties in a
very different way. Confirming some of your deepest suspicions is part
of what this day is about.

27 SUNDAY
Moon Age Day 23 • Moon Sign Taurus

am...

pm...
It may be best to take a secondary role when it comes to the more
practical aspects of life, even though in your heart you know that your
own way of doing things is the best one. Allowing others to believe that
they have some input is not a mistake and can lead to greater co-
operation on their part.

← *NEGATIVE TREND*						*POSITIVE TREND* →				
-5	-4	-3	-2	-1		+1	+2	+3	+4	+5
					LOVE					
					MONEY					
					LUCK					
					VITALITY					

28 MONDAY
Moon Age Day 24 • Moon Sign Taurus

am ....

pm ....
Any highlights today are likely to be associated with your social life,
which looks especially good at the present time. You can make much out
of events the casual offers that are coming in from outside and will also
want to make the most favourable impression on those around you that
you can. The effort is worthwhile.

29 TUESDAY
Moon Age Day 25 • Moon Sign Gemini

am ....

pm ....
You will not be talked out of anything that you have got firmly into your
head at present, even though in your heart you may realise that on
occasions you are quite capable of being wrong. A comfortable period is
hardly likely today, but don't allow this to divert you from paths that you
have chosen so carefully.

30 WEDNESDAY
Moon Age Day 26 • Moon Sign Gemini

am ....

pm ....
Certain actions that you take today show that there are occasions when
you can be your own worst enemy. Routines take over from a more
intense personal period and you react according to your own conscience
in most situations. Putting additional pressure on yourself would not be
helpful at this time.

31 THURSDAY
Moon Age Day 27 • Moon Sign Gemini

am ....

pm ....
A day to be careful, since there is the possibility of slight mishaps,
especially in your home. Out in the world you are bright and cheerful,
anxious to do whatever you can to be of help to others and essentially
cheerful in your attitude. Convention is something that you really do not
care for the look of now.

1 FRIDAY

Moon Age Day 28 • Moon Sign Cancer

am..

pm..
Certain emotional issues from the past now have the power to grab your attention and can make you look back, rather than forward. Although there might be some sense in learning from experience, this is really not the best time to be trying to change what you already are, unless of course you are certain about your facts.

2 SATURDAY

Moon Age Day 29 • Moon Sign Cancer

am..

pm..
You can find yourself drawn into arguments that are not of your own making today, and could easily discover that you are wedged between people who fail to see eye to eye. In any situation of this sort it is very important to remain as impartial as you can and not to allow yourself to be forced into taking sides.

3 SUNDAY

Moon Age Day 0 • Moon Sign Leo

am..

pm..
Your self confidence is now on the increase, a fact that allows you to look forward in a positive sense and something that you will want to use to your advantage whenever you can. Plan your finances carefully and don't allow yourself to be held back by the negative attitudes of friends or relations.

← NEGATIVE TREND							POSITIVE TREND →			
-5	-4	-3	-2	-1			+1	+2	+3	+4	+5
					LOVE					
					MONEY					
					LUCK					
					VITALITY					

YOUR MONTH AT A GLANCE

The twelve numbered boxes represent the important areas in your life. The key to the numbers you will find beneath the panel. A sun above the number indicates that opportunities are around. A cloud below the number, that you should be a bit defensive. Nothing above or below and life will be pretty ordinary.

1	2	3	4	5	6	7	8	9	10	11	12

KEY

1 Strength of Personality
2 Personal Finance
3 Useful Information Gathering
4 Domestic Affairs
5 Pleasure & Romance
6 Effective Work & Health

7 One to One Relationships
8 Questioning, Thinking & Deciding
9 External Influences / Education
10 Career Aspirations
11 Teamwork Activities
12 Unconscious Impulses

AUGUST HIGHS AND LOWS

Here, I show how the rhythm of the Moon will affect you this month. Like the tide, your energies and abilities will rise and fall with its pattern. When it is above the date line, go-for-it. When it is below the line you should be resting.

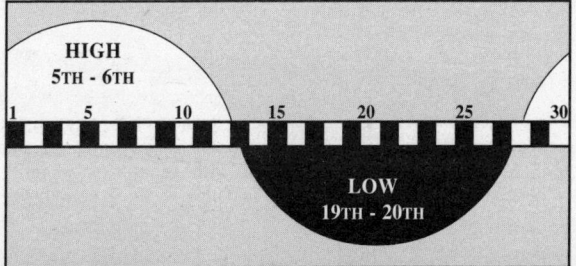

4 MONDAY
Moon Age Day 1 • Moon Sign Leo

am ....

pm ....
Put off any major decision making until tomorrow and do what you can to view today as a transitional period. This might mean that you feel you are not getting much done, but you can at least sit back and look at life a little more fully than might have been the case of late. Interesting social diversions are likely.

5 TUESDAY
Moon Age Day 2 • Moon Sign Virgo

am ....

pm ....
Now the time is right to move forward positively, and to make the most of the lunar high. There are gains to be made through general good luck, through relationships and also with regard to long-term career planning. You may not have time to take a breath at the moment, but you should enjoy yourself!

6 WEDNESDAY
Moon Age Day 3 • Moon Sign Virgo

am ....

pm ....
You should really have Lady Luck on your side at the moment and may also find that providence smiles on you in ways that have no financial content at all. Not really a time to hedge your bets in the typical Virgo fashion, but rather a period when you need to let out all the stops and trust life to support you.

7 THURSDAY
Moon Age Day 4 • Moon Sign Virgo

am ....

pm ....
You are very accommodating regarding the wishes of people around you at present and can get on well with just about anyone. A time for thinking about getting yourself involved with groups or societies that have not figured before and you should find this to be a period when co-operation at all levels is useful.

8 FRIDAY   *Moon Age Day 5 • Moon Sign Libra*

am..

pm..
You probably get an easy ride through life today, though that does not mean that you can afford to sit back and do nothing. You need to be looking at possibilities for much later in the month, and especially the period around the 23rd. If you have been off colour of late, the situation should improve.

9 SATURDAY   *Moon Age Day 6 • Moon Sign Libra*

am..

pm..
Although there may be a few personal pressures about at the moment, these are not likely to last all that long. Activities of many different sorts are likely to take your fancy at this time and you do plenty to support those around you. A good day for taking a little time out to watch the flowers grow.

10 SUNDAY   *Moon Age Day 7 • Moon Sign Scorpio*

am..

pm..
A quicker and more immediate pace seems to develop so that, despite the arrival of Sunday, you certainly have plenty to do. Probably a good time to delegate and to allow others to carry some of the load that would otherwise be placed on your shoulders. Not really a time for trying to 'go it alone' too much!

← NEGATIVE TREND						POSITIVE TREND →				
-5	-4	-3	-2	-1		+1	+2	+3	+4	+5
					LOVE					
					MONEY					
					LUCK					
					VITALITY					

11 MONDAY
Moon Age Day 8 • Moon Sign Scorpio

am..

pm..
You really are quite keen to get whatever you can from life in material terms at the moment and could be accused by certain other people of being slightly 'grabbing'. Of course this isn't the case is it? In reality you are simply looking out for your own interests. You might have to make this plain to someone.

12 TUESDAY
Moon Age Day 9 • Moon Sign Scorpio

am..

pm..
You should be looking and feeling at your best now and can make a good impression on the world at large. Not everyone comes good for you at present, though it is only a matter of time before you are able to bring even the most awkward people round to your way of thinking. Find time to sort out a nagging problem.

13 WEDNESDAY
Moon Age Day 10 • Moon Sign Sagittarius

am..

pm..
A time when you should consolidate present plans and when you could find that a few positive chickens are coming home to roost. There are one or two frustrations to be dealt with and these are best looked at early in the day, leaving time later to please yourself. You expect a great deal of yourself now.

14 THURSDAY
Moon Age Day 11 • Moon Sign Sagittarius

am..

pm..
Home and domestic life may look a little low key right now and if this is the case you could do with injecting a little effort into situations to get them back on line. People generally may seem to be taking less notice of you than you would wish, though it is only a matter of time before you realise that the reverse is true.

15 FRIDAY
Moon Age Day 12 • Moon Sign Capricorn

am..

pm..
You may have to guard against some outspoken tendencies, which in one way or another come as a direct contradiction to what happened yesterday. Life is bound to be a little up and down right now and you should not allow this fact to get you down in any way. After all, variety really is the spice of life!

16 SATURDAY
Moon Age Day 13 • Moon Sign Capricorn

am..

pm..
Thoughts of romance enter your mind and there is everything to play for in the personal stakes at present. Your ego is helped by the fact that those around you appear to have a higher opinion of you at present and as a result you can go far in a general sense. Probably not a good day for gambling however.

17 SUNDAY
Moon Age Day 14 • Moon Sign Aquarius

am..

pm..
Some of your more typical Virgoan traits are enhanced by what the planets do for you right now. This is generally a good thing, just as long as you do not allow your stubborn streak to gain the upper hand. Be a little careful generally because it would be all too easy to run out of steam at present.

← *NEGATIVE TREND*						*POSITIVE TREND*	→			
-5	-4	-3	-2	-1		+1	+2	+3	+4	+5
					LOVE					
					MONEY					
					LUCK					
					VITALITY					

18 MONDAY   *Moon Age Day 15 • Moon Sign Aquarius*

am ....

pm ....
Being rather more likely to find yourself influenced by others at the moment, you do need to make certain that what they are saying and doing genuinely makes sense. You might find the start of this working week brings responsibilities that you have not looked for but don't turn them away without a decent review.

19 TUESDAY   *Moon Age Day 16 • Moon Sign Pisces*

am ....

pm ....
As the Moon moves into your opposite sign, dig yourself in for a couple of much quieter days than of late. Fill your spare time by doing the sort of quiet things that take your fancy, but do not expect to move any mountains professionally speaking. Why not just contemplate the possibility of having a rest.

20 WEDNESDAY   *Moon Age Day 17 • Moon Sign Pisces*

am ....

pm ....
It would be best to allow your partner, or other trusted parties to have their way at present. You really do not want to involve yourself in too much decision making and can be certain to withdraw into yourself at the first sign of friction. By tomorrow you return to normal, until then just relax.

21 THURSDAY   *Moon Age Day 18 • Moon Sign Aries*

am ....

pm ....
There are certain significant moves that you can make at the moment that will turn to your advantage later. Slow and steady wins the race and so you should not try to force any sort of issue or to push the bounds of the possible too far ahead of yourself. An overwhelming optimism overtakes you now.

22 FRIDAY
Moon Age Day 19 • Moon Sign Aries

am ....

pm ....
Communications do not do you any favours at the moment and it is very important indeed to listen to what others are actually saying. You could easily get hold of the wrong end of the stick, and this will only mean that you have to work all the harder to put things right later. Your boredom threshold is low.

23 SATURDAY
Moon Age Day 20 • Moon Sign Taurus

am ....

pm ....
The Sun sails majestically into your solar first house, opening up a really dynamic period in your life and making this the most important day of the month. Remember however, that this is a month long trend during which you make much more of your own, true potential. A time to look and plan ahead carefully.

24 SUNDAY
Moon Age Day 21 • Moon Sign Taurus

am ....

pm ....
You might not think that your ideas have much weight in the minds of important people who surround you. Some Virgoans are likely to be a little cynical at the moment and you could do with making certain that you are not one of them. You really can afford to take life at face value and should be willing to do so.

← NEGATIVE TREND							POSITIVE TREND →				
-5	-4	-3	-2	-1			+1	+2	+3	+4	+5
					LOVE						
					MONEY						
					LUCK						
					VITALITY						

25 MONDAY
Moon Age Day 22 • Moon Sign Gemini

am ....

pm ....
This must represent a day of happiness and fulfilment in one way or
another and is a possible turning point where your professional plans are
concerned. Be willing to speak out and to allow what others are saying
to play a part in your thinking too. A day of intellectual and general co-
operation.

26 TUESDAY
Moon Age Day 23 • Moon Sign Gemini

am ....

pm ....
Whilst others are now more than willing to take your ideas seriously, you
could have a few doubts about them yourself. Try to do your best to take
yourself seriously, though probably not too much so. It is easy to laugh
at the moment, which can surely never be considered to be a bad thing.

27 WEDNESDAY
Moon Age Day 24 • Moon Sign Gemini

am ....

pm ....
If you concentrate all your effort on your own ideas now you are almost
certain to come unstuck. Even the most unlikely directions offer the
possibility of bringing new schemes into your mind and you will only kick
yourself if you haven't been listening. There are some surprises in store
later.

28 THURSDAY
Moon Age Day 25 • Moon Sign Cancer

am ....

pm ....
The best part of August for travel, so that those amongst you who are
already on holiday have clearly made the right choice. This trend lasts
a while, so even if you cannot alter your schedule for today you might find
the weekend to be a good potential time for getting away from home and
off into the great outdoors.

29 FRIDAY
Moon Age Day 26 • Moon Sign Cancer

am..

pm..
Always having the longer-term in view, you now find yourself happy to go with the flow for a day or two. You probably have good reason to feel a little smug about some of your actions and will be also willing to give relatives a fair hearing. A balanced Virgo greets the arrival of the weekend.

30 SATURDAY
Moon Age Day 27 • Moon Sign Leo

am..

pm..
Did you decide to opt for a change of scene? If the answer is yes then you have made the right move. Whatever you decide to do today, make certain that at least part of it is fulfilling for you personally. Confidence does not feel to be especially high at first, but should improve as the day wears on.

31 SUNDAY
Moon Age Day 28 • Moon Sign Leo

am..

pm..
You are used to reacting to situations fairly quickly and your mind jumps to conclusions all the time. This turns out to be a very good thing just now and you should find today has much to offer as a result. Creating more space for yourself could appeal to you, but don't be held back by negative thinking types.

← *NEGATIVE TREND*							*POSITIVE TREND* →			
-5	-4	-3	-2	-1		+1	+2	+3	+4	+5
					LOVE					
					MONEY					
					LUCK					
					VITALITY					

1997

YOUR MONTH AT A GLANCE

The twelve numbered boxes represent the important areas in your life. The key to the numbers you will find beneath the panel. A sun above the number indicates that opportunities are around. A cloud below the number, that you should be a bit defensive. Nothing above or below and life will be pretty ordinary.

1	2	3	4	5	6	7	8	9	10	11	12

KEY

1 Strength of Personality
2 Personal Finance
3 Useful Information Gathering
4 Domestic Affairs
5 Pleasure & Romance
6 Effective Work & Health

7 One to One Relationships
8 Questioning, Thinking & Deciding
9 External Influences / Education
10 Career Aspirations
11 Teamwork Activities
12 Unconscious Impulses

SEPTEMBER HIGHS AND LOWS

Here, I show how the rhythm of the Moon will affect you this month. Like the tide, your energies and abilities will rise and fall with its pattern. When it is above the date line, go-for-it. When it is below the line you should be resting.

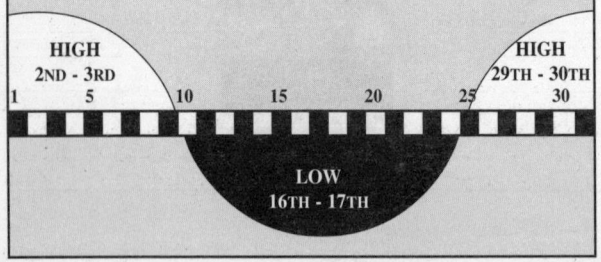

HIGH
2ND - 3RD

HIGH
29TH - 30TH

LOW
16TH - 17TH

1 MONDAY

Moon Age Day 0 • Moon Sign Leo

am ....

pm ....
Along comes September and aren't you just ready for its arrival? All in all you should find this to be a stimulating month with a fine start. Any Monday morning blues should soon disappear and you have plenty to keep you occupied today. Your natural wisdom is to hand and turns out to be useful.

2 TUESDAY

Moon Age Day 1 • Moon Sign Virgo

am ....

pm ....
The lunar high is upon you and that means that the world can be your oyster at the moment. There is really no need to hold back in any direction and everything to play for in an hour by hour sense. All you have to remember is to tackle one job at once and not to run yourself ragged. Plans made now should materialise.

3 WEDNESDAY

Moon Age Day 2 • Moon Sign Virgo

am ....

pm ....
Your carefully planned work is under attack from one direction or another. Remember though that the lunar high is still with you and also that you do not have to accept the point of view that someone else puts forward simply because it is there on the table. In all probability your intuition is your best guide.

4 THURSDAY

Moon Age Day 3 • Moon Sign Libra

am ....

pm ....
Your confidence appears to be very high today, perhaps just a little too much so for your own good. Try to make certain that you have your facts right because it would be all too easy to come unstuck simply because you have not paid sufficient attention to details. A friend has some interesting news.

5 FRIDAY

Moon Age Day 4 • Moon Sign Libra

am..

pm..
Be careful how you use resources at the moment. It isn't that you have
to restrict yourself in any way, merely that you require a thinking
approach to life and what it offers. Not a good time to gamble, unless you
are certain that your intuition agrees with your common sense. Try not
to push yourself too hard.

6 SATURDAY

Moon Age Day 5 • Moon Sign Libra

am..

pm..
Whilst you can expect most trends to swing your way today, there are a
number of frustrations to be dealt with, mainly coming from the
direction of friends and relatives. Acting on impulse does not work in
your favour at the moment and it would be sensible to sit back and take
stock of all possibilities.

7 SUNDAY

Moon Age Day 6 • Moon Sign Scorpio

am..

pm..
Positive thinking can move mountains right now, so that although you
may have found yesterday to be slightly frustrating things are now
improving, almost beyond belief. When it comes to a new professional
project, don't take your eye off the ball and avoid passing your own
responsibilities across to others.

← NEGATIVE TREND								POSITIVE TREND →				
-5	-4	-3	-2	-1				+1	+2	+3	+4	+5
					LOVE							
					MONEY							
					LUCK							
					VITALITY							

8 MONDAY

Moon Age Day 7 • Moon Sign Scorpio

am...

pm...
You can benefit slightly in a financial sense, so that although this could not be considered to be a key day, it does have much in its favour. A free and easy attitude to life and love makes you attractive in the eyes of those around you and makes it worthwhile sticking your neck out just a little.

9 TUESDAY

Moon Age Day 8 • Moon Sign Sagittarius

am...

pm...
It seems that some jobs never end, and on top of everything else you are expected to remain committed and cheerful. Just do it! Today is the sort of period when what you appear to be turns out to be what you actually are, so you cannot lose anything by remaining positive and hopeful with regard to the future.

10 WEDNESDAY

Moon Age Day 9 • Moon Sign Sagittarius

am...

pm...
You should enjoy the very active role that you offer yourself today and you can find that people flock around to lend a helping hand at just the right time. You might be feeling rather jaded at first, though as the hours past your energy is renewed and your vision of the possible increases beyond belief.

11 THURSDAY

Moon Age Day 10 • Moon Sign Sagittarius

am...

pm...
Ego energy is still fairly high and you should have few or no doubts about your own abilities right now. React according to your intuition, which is unlikely to let you down at any stage this month. Routines have to be dealt with but for some reason they are now less likely to get on your nerves.

12 FRIDAY
Moon Age Day 11 • Moon Sign Capricorn

am..

pm..
A brief phase when your ability to get on with those around you goes out through the roof. You are generally quite personable in any case, but you can take advantage of present trends by simply being willing to say whatever you feel to be right, no matter who it is you find yourself talking to.

13 SATURDAY
Moon Age Day 12 • Moon Sign Capricorn

am..

pm..
Your sharp eye takes everything in, your quick brain assesses it and your ready tongue finds the right response. This is a time to trust yourself to the hilt and not to allow yourself to be duped by the glib tongues of others. Life throws a few strange characters into your path for the next couple of days.

14 SUNDAY
Moon Age Day 13 • Moon Sign Aquarius

am..

pm..
A day that should see you busier than ever, even though this being Sunday you might have been looking for a quieter interlude. There are gains to be made in a personal sense, and quite a few people around who are more than willing to join you in an adventure of some sort. Critics are few and far between.

← NEGATIVE TREND						POSITIVE TREND →				
-5	-4	-3	-2	-1		+1	+2	+3	+4	+5
					LOVE					
					MONEY					
					LUCK					
					VITALITY					

15 MONDAY
Moon Age Day 14 • Moon Sign Aquarius

am...

pm...
You need to have something of a quieter interlude and as the Moon gradually moves to its opposite position in your chart, so things do tend to slow down a little. If you are wise, you can take the opportunity of stopping to take stock. Not a day for pushing the limits of the credible much further than you have to.

16 TUESDAY
Moon Age Day 15 • Moon Sign Pisces

am...

pm...
It probably feels as if many of your plans are waiting in the wings today, another fact that is down to the present position of the Moon. All the same it would be better to be patient than to risk making mistakes and there should be plenty of time later for a more enterprising and generally successful push.

17 WEDNESDAY
Moon Age Day 16 • Moon Sign Pisces

am...

pm...
Whilst the planetary influences today bring you to a sense of general optimism regarding your life as a whole, it is in the area of personal relationships that you notice the best trends developing. There are gains to be made as a result, not least of all in terms of the view you have of yourself at present.

18 THURSDAY
Moon Age Day 17 • Moon Sign Aries

am...

pm...
You should find it fairly easy to make any important changes, especially at work. With plenty of other people in the same frame of mind you should not find it difficult to enlist support for almost any new plan. A different sort of day is on the cards and one that relies a great deal on acting intuitively.

19 FRIDAY
Moon Age Day 18 • Moon Sign Aries

am ....

pm ....
Keep your life just as varied as you wish it to be. You won't find other people at all difficult to come to terms with and, once again, they seem more than willing to help you out if they can. You are likely to be planning an excursion or perhaps a visit for the weekend, and looking at work next week too.

20 SATURDAY
Moon Age Day 19 • Moon Sign Taurus

am ....

pm ....
You are likely to want to have your say now, no matter what others think about the fact. This quality of Virgo rises to the fore now and again and simply has to be toned down a little if you want the sort of co-operation of the last couple of months to continue. It is clear that not everyone is quite in tune with you.

21 SUNDAY
Moon Age Day 20 • Moon Sign Taurus

am ....

pm ....
It's time to keep going and to let your family members know that you are there if they need you. Someone you haven't seen for quite a while makes a renewed appearance in your life and brings with them some good ideas that you may want to look at carefully. The attitude presented by your partner takes some understanding.

← NEGATIVE TREND						POSITIVE TREND →				
-5	-4	-3	-2	-1		+1	+2	+3	+4	+5
					LOVE					
					MONEY					
					LUCK					
					VITALITY					

22 MONDAY
Moon Age Day 21 • Moon Sign Gemini

am ....

pm ....
A mix and match sort of start to the week, but none the less interesting
for that. Something that you put forward as a plan last week now looks
as if it is going to work out to your advantage and you should be more
than happy about the fact. Don't hold yourself back in personal discussions later.

23 TUESDAY
Moon Age Day 22 • Moon Sign Gemini

am ....

pm ....
Renewed confidence makes it easier for you to get your own way, and
without treading on the toes of other people. There are some real
characters about at present and you will be pleased to take them into
your confidence. An attractive Virgoan is on offer at the moment and you
have energy to spare for all projects.

24 WEDNESDAY
Moon Age Day 23 • Moon Sign Cancer

am ....

pm ....
A day when you can very easily bring out the best in others and when
they find it easy to understand what makes you tick. Plan your moves
for the 2nd or 3rd of next month now and make certain that you are
looking ahead generally. Someone who has been awkward to deal with
of late now comes good again.

25 THURSDAY
Moon Age Day 24 • Moon Sign Cancer

am ....

pm ....
There may be differences of opinion developing, especially within the
family. These are going to take some dealing with and it might be quite
sensible to leave certain plans on the back burner until you are certain
that you have personal relationships sorted out once and for all. A
neutral mediator might be the answer.

26 FRIDAY
Moon Age Day 25 • Moon Sign Leo

am..

pm..
This is likely to be a rather hectic period as far as you are concerned. It could be that you are simply trying to get as much done as you can ahead of the weekend, or that you do not have the time to fit everything in. Whatever the truth of the situation, you are going to have to compartment your life at present.

27 SATURDAY
Moon Age Day 26 • Moon Sign Leo

am..

pm..
Avoid looking at the world through rose coloured glasses today. This being Saturday, you might have more time to think about things, but that does not mean allowing yourself to dwell of situations more than you should. A practical approach really does work the best, both now and for some days to come.

28 SUNDAY
Moon Age Day 27 • Moon Sign Leo

am..

pm..
The day speeds up as it gets older and you should feel that your level of energy is once again on the increase. This is the last opportunity for two or three days to spend some time thinking about inconsequential matters and for musing only about what appeals to you. Take the chance whilst you can.

← *NEGATIVE TREND*   *POSITIVE TREND* →

-5	-4	-3	-2	-1			+1	+2	+3	+4	+5
					LOVE						
					MONEY						
					LUCK						
					VITALITY						

154

29 MONDAY   *Moon Age Day 28 • Moon Sign Virgo*

am..

pm..
A physical peak when you feel on top form and able to deal with just
about anything that comes your way. Organising your time is important,
so that you can fit in just about everything of importance. With a bit of
luck someone fairly close might fail to notice that you are late getting
something important done.

30 TUESDAY   *Moon Age Day 29 • Moon Sign Virgo*

am..

pm..
The lunar high is still with you, of that fact there is really no doubt. It
would be sensible to pace yourself a little because you are inclined to
expect rather a lot of yourself at this time. All the same, you have plenty
of energy to spare, a rather jolly outlook on life and charm enough
socially.

1 WEDNESDAY   *Moon Age Day 0 • Moon Sign Libra*

am..

pm..
The emphasis today seems to be on luxury and self-indulgence, which is
a resort that all Virgo people have to visit now and again. There are some
rather strange attitudes about coming from the direction of others and
all you can really do is to wait and see how they will react in the fullness
of time.

2 THURSDAY   *Moon Age Day 1 • Moon Sign Libra*

am..

pm..
Your earning power is now certainly on the increase and this might be
due to the fact that you have been willing to ask for a rise, or to take on
more than will have been the case previously. There is also a possibility
that you are simply being seen in a more favourable light and are being
elevated as a result.

3 FRIDAY
Moon Age Day 2 • Moon Sign Libra

am...

pm...
Plan your schedules as carefully as you can today, and hold back if you
think that too much pressure is being placed upon you. There are details
to be sorted out and many facts of life do not appear to be working out
strictly as you would wish or intend now. Creating the right sort of
atmosphere at home is important.

4 SATURDAY
Moon Age Day 3 • Moon Sign Scorpio

am...

pm...
There are various obstacles being thrown in your path at the moment,
not least of all the fact that Saturday brings a period when it is slightly
difficult to get exactly what you want from life. This might come down
to the fact that whilst you are away from work, you have to concentrate
instead on domestic matters.

5 SUNDAY
Moon Age Day 4 • Moon Sign Scorpio

am...

pm...
You may have to overcome some fence-sitting tendencies, especially
where domestic matters are concerned. It should not be long however
before you find yourself more into the swing of home life and the
demands it makes of you. Confidence is everything to you and appears
to be on the increase again.

← *NEGATIVE TREND*								*POSITIVE TREND*	→	
-5	-4	-3	-2	-1		+1	+2	+3	+4	+5
					LOVE					
					MONEY					
					LUCK					
					VITALITY					

YOUR MONTH AT A GLANCE

The twelve numbered boxes represent the important areas in your life.
The key to the numbers you will find beneath the panel. A sun above the
number indicates that opportunities are around. A cloud below the
number, that you should be a bit defensive. Nothing above or below and
life will be pretty ordinary.

1	2	3	4	5	6	7	8	9	10	11	12

OCTOBER HIGHS AND LOWS

Here, I show how the rhythm of the Moon will affect you this month. Like
the tide, your energies and abilities will rise and fall with its pattern.
When it is above the date line, go-for-it. When it is below the line you
should be resting.

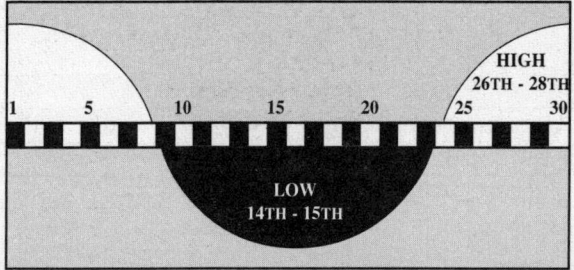

6 MONDAY
Moon Age Day 5 • Moon Sign Sagittarius

am ....

pm ....
Opt for a change of pace if it proves possible to do so. With less of an emphasis placed upon work for once, and more of your time being devoted to personal matters, romance begins to play a bigger role in your thinking too. Rules and regulations are not so easy to deal with, though arguing about them may not help.

7 TUESDAY
Moon Age Day 6 • Moon Sign Sagittarius

am ....

pm ....
Though certain family matters tend to be rather irksome, you have to deal with them as best you can. The time needed to do so could divert you from more pressing professional matters and could prevent you from making some of the headway that you had hoped for so near the start of this working week.

8 WEDNESDAY
Moon Age Day 7 • Moon Sign Sagittarius

am ....

pm ....
Social and romantic prospects look especially good, and probably better than you remember them being for weeks. If there is a problem here it is likely to lie in the fact that you have so very much to do that you cannot possibly fit everything into what is already a busy life. Choices do need to be made.

9 THURSDAY
Moon Age Day 8 • Moon Sign Capricorn

am ....

pm ....
Some Virgoans will feel totally drained of energy at present. If you are one of them it could be that you are not exactly tired with life as a whole, but simply with a certain aspect of it. The time is right to turn your attention in other directions, and to ring the changes, especially in a domestic sense.

10 FRIDAY

Moon Age Day 9 • Moon Sign Capricorn

am..

pm..
Your general judgements have rarely been better than you notice them
to be right now, so you can afford to back your own hunches up to the hilt.
Where a mystery cops up, you will be more than happy to work it out for
yourself and should even take great delight in having the possibility of
doing so.

11 SATURDAY

Moon Age Day 10 • Moon Sign Aquarius

am..

pm..
A favourable day for meetings of almost any sort, and especially those
that relate to your family in some way. Perhaps you may be thinking
about an outing, or even a weekend away. Most of the individuals you
come across should be in the right frame of mind to take your opinions
on board.

12 SUNDAY

Moon Age Day 11 • Moon Sign Aquarius

am..

pm..
Positive and encouraging news is yours for the taking, though you will
have to ensure that you are in the right place at the right time to hear
it. Even apparent gossip can play its part in giving you a multitude of
ideas for the future and all you have to do is to talk others round to your
point of view.

← NEGATIVE TREND						POSITIVE TREND →				
-5	-4	-3	-2	-1			+1	+2	+3	+4	+5
					LOVE						
					MONEY						
					LUCK						
					VITALITY						

13 MONDAY
Moon Age Day 12 • Moon Sign Pisces

am ....

pm ....
It's true that you start out the day by being curious or even sceptical regarding the motives of other people. All the same, before long you should come to realise that they are pulling in the same direction as you are and do genuinely want to help. Confusion does not play an important role later in the day.

14 TUESDAY
Moon Age Day 13 • Moon Sign Pisces

am ....

pm ....
There is a lull in daily affairs, and in the sort of excitement that you are apt to take for granted. This is probably not a bad thing at all, especially if it offers you the personal alternatives, such as putting your feet up once work is out of the way. Listen to what life is trying to tell you.

15 WEDNESDAY
Moon Age Day 14 • Moon Sign Aries

am ....

pm ....
There is a truth today and that is that you fool yourself if you think that you can keep up a hectic pace whilst some negative aspects exist around you. This is an ideal time to be planning and scheming. Once you realise the fact, all is well and your friends turn out to be quite accommodating.

16 THURSDAY
Moon Age Day 15 • Moon Sign Aries

am ....

pm ....
Don't allow slightly disturbed moods to have a bearing on personal relationships and the way that they are apt to turn out at the moment. There is a tendency for you to take trips down memory lane, which is not necessarily a bad thing, as long as your judgement remains in the present. Confidence grows later.

17 FRIDAY

Moon Age Day 16 • Moon Sign Taurus

am...

pm...
Some slightly unfortunate planetary aspects in your chart at present can cause you to feel a little out of sorts, making it easy for opponents to score points at your expense. Of course this is only a problem if you consider that there is some sort of competition taking place, which in reality there may not be.

18 SATURDAY

Moon Age Day 17 • Moon Sign Taurus

am...

pm...
A steady start to the weekend, at least it should be. The trouble is that there are opposing factors in your chart at the moment, so that while one set of aspects is telling you to stop and think, other planetary positions are urging you onward. The positive ones win out, which is why this becomes a key day.

19 SUNDAY

Moon Age Day 18 • Moon Sign Gemini

am...

pm...
Now in a dynamic phase, you still retain the patience that encourages your more adventurous and dynamic nature. Use it today because you will achieve far more by taking the positive qualities of the present time and utilising them slowly and steadily. On a Sunday you may have little other choice.

← *NEGATIVE TREND*						*POSITIVE TREND* →				
-5	-4	-3	-2	-1		+1	+2	+3	+4	+5
					LOVE					
					MONEY					
					LUCK					
					VITALITY					

20 MONDAY
Moon Age Day 19 • Moon Sign Gemini

am ....

pm ....
The wheels of general progress are turning positively as far as you are concerned, though you might be over concerned at the moment with a particular problem. It will be no bad thing to stay in the dark regarding specific issues at the beginning of this working week. Be patient and everything will work out.

21 TUESDAY
Moon Age Day 20 • Moon Sign Cancer

am ....

pm ....
With a slight possibility of misunderstandings cropping up, do make certain that you express yourself as clearly as you can. Although you may be doing your best to please everyone, it won't be possible to do so. There should be some especially happy times by the evening, though possibly home-based ones.

22 WEDNESDAY
Moon Age Day 21 • Moon Sign Cancer

am ....

pm ....
Partners can be quite demanding at this stage of the working week, though most of your attention needs to be turned towards career prospects and general practicalities. When faced with a number of uncertainties, you may be inclined to opt for situations that are steady and with which you are familiar.

23 THURSDAY
Moon Age Day 22 • Moon Sign Cancer

am ....

pm ....
The Sun is now entering your solar third house, offering you better powers of communication and bringing a month long period when it should be easy for you to get your message across. It should be simplicity now just to speak your mind, in the almost certain knowledge that your point of view is being considered.

24 FRIDAY
Moon Age Day 23 • Moon Sign Leo

am...

pm...
You tend to do exactly what you want today, and should not be distracted by specific people who appear to know your business better than you do. On the whole this should be a fairly interesting time and may bring more in the way of financial gains than you have been expecting. Make decisions quickly.

25 SATURDAY
Moon Age Day 24 • Moon Sign Leo

am...

pm...
In personal attachments it could be difficult to get your own way, which is why a more casual sort of mixing seems to be preferred at present. You can see the faults in others all too easily and it would probably be more sensible to recognise their strengths instead. Who knows, they might help you out?

26 SUNDAY
Moon Age Day 25 • Moon Sign Virgo

am...

pm...
A time for fresh plans and for a revolutionary new way of looking at old situations. Be prepared to be flexible at this time and don't allow any hiccups of a personal nature to have a bearing on your thinking in the long-term. The lunar high on Sunday is difficult to steer, but your incentives remain intact.

← NEGATIVE TREND						POSITIVE TREND →				
-5	-4	-3	-2	-1		+1	+2	+3	+4	+5
					LOVE					
					MONEY					
					LUCK					
					VITALITY					

27 MONDAY
Moon Age Day 26 • Moon Sign Virgo

am ....

pm ....
This is a day to organise your social and sporting life, probably trying out the sort of new incentive and idea that will stand you in good stead for considerably longer than just today. Any restrictions early in the day are soon dealt with and you really can make the most of the period whilst the Moon favours you.

28 TUESDAY
Moon Age Day 27 • Moon Sign Virgo

am ....

pm ....
Press ahead with practical and professional issues and leave the more social qualities of the day until later. There is no reason why you should not put a definite plan of action to the test this week, though this is a long-term potential and demands that you concentrate your efforts in the same direction for several days.

29 WEDNESDAY
Moon Age Day 28 • Moon Sign Libra

am ....

pm ....
It's possible that today you are looking for the chance to work hand in hand with like-minded types, no matter if that is with regard to domestic matters or perhaps even social ones. You get yourself into the swing of things much more readily than you did last week and feel new incentives around you at every turn.

30 THURSDAY
Moon Age Day 29 • Moon Sign Libra

am ....

pm ....
Finding compromise is difficult just for the moment, mainly because it is others who are unwilling to look at situations in the same way that you do. Of course, from your side of the fence it looks as though they are being rather unreasonable, whilst they probably have the same opinion of you.

31 FRIDAY
Moon Age Day 0 • Moon Sign Scorpio

am...

pm...
The things that you don't really want to do tend to be left alone today, whilst those tasks that appeal to you are nothing more or less than a labour of love. Even the most casual of situations socially or romantically can have great implications and you should be willing to plan now for the weekend to come.

1 SATURDAY
Moon Age Day 1 • Moon Sign Scorpio

am...

pm...
Invitations generally now begin to take on an importance that they may not have done previously. There is much to be gained from accepting offers, and from making the most of them once you have. Family outings or simply the chance to talk to relatives would be not only fun but carry advantages.

2 SUNDAY
Moon Age Day 2 • Moon Sign Scorpio

am...

pm...
Be prepared to win others round socially, simply by being your own charming self. Without really having to put all that much hard work, the world can seem to be your oyster right now. It's possible that you are suffering a little from fatigue though and so you do need some moments in which to unwind.

← *NEGATIVE TREND*							*POSITIVE TREND* →				
-5	-4	-3	-2	-1			+1	+2	+3	+4	+5
					LOVE						
					MONEY						
					LUCK						
					VITALITY						

1997

YOUR MONTH AT A GLANCE

The twelve numbered boxes represent the important areas in your life.
The key to the numbers you will find beneath the panel. A sun above the
number indicates that opportunities are around. A cloud below the
number, that you should be a bit defensive. Nothing above or below and
life will be pretty ordinary.

1	2	3	4	5	6	7	8	9	10	11	12

KEY

1 Strength of Personality
2 Personal Finance
3 Useful Information Gathering
4 Domestic Affairs
5 Pleasure & Romance
6 Effective Work & Health
7 One to One Relationships
8 Questioning, Thinking & Deciding
9 External Influences / Education
10 Career Aspirations
11 Teamwork Activities
12 Unconscious Impulses

NOVEMBER HIGHS AND LOWS

Here, I show how the rhythm of the Moon will affect you this month. Like
the tide, your energies and abilities will rise and fall with its pattern.
When it is above the date line, go-for-it. When it is below the line you
should be resting.

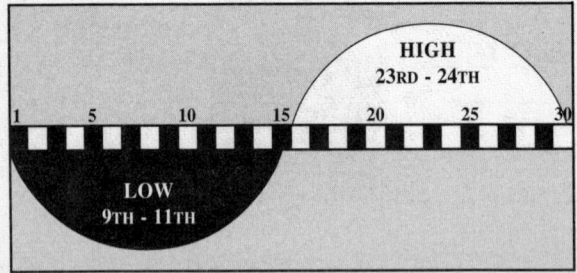

HIGH
23RD - 24TH

LOW
9TH - 11TH

3 MONDAY
Moon Age Day 3 • Moon Sign Sagittarius

am ....

pm ....
The power of your opinions is so great at the moment that there is little
chance of others failing to understand how you feel. This is unlikely to
lead to rows though since you have a great ability at the moment to put
your point of view in a positive way. Now is the time to push forward in
many ways.

4 TUESDAY
Moon Age Day 4 • Moon Sign Sagittarius

am ....

pm ....
You probably would prefer to stay at home today and the world outside
might look less than inviting for some reason. Spend as much time as
you can in the bosom of your family and take what you can from personal
relationships. These look especially settled at present and have much to
offer you.

5 WEDNESDAY
Moon Age Day 5 • Moon Sign Capricorn

am ....

pm ....
Spirit raising enterprises come along and lift the quality of the day much
more than you will be expecting. You will amaze yourself with all that
you manage to do and do need to concentrate on the job in hand. By the
evening the chances are that you will be tired but satisfied with your
efforts.

6 THURSDAY
Moon Age Day 6 • Moon Sign Capricorn

am ....

pm ....
In some ways you have been rather tense and restless recently and these
trends probably disappear as today wears on. As a result the world will
see a much more relaxed sort of Virgoan and you find that you have more
time to spend with the people who you care about the most. Give yourself
a little treat now.

7 FRIDAY
Moon Age Day 7 • Moon Sign Aquarius

am..

pm..
After a time of lurching from one extreme to another your life is now more
settled and generally interesting. Although there is little about today
that could be called exciting, it deserves to be judged as a key day because
there is so much potential towards success. Most people have your best
interests at heart.

8 SATURDAY
Moon Age Day 8 • Moon Sign Aquarius

am..

pm..
An excellent period for all romantic matters. Someone in the know is
able to help you boost your relationship prospects and you should not be
too surprised if attention is being paid to you which comes from fairly
unexpected directions. Your enthusiasm for life has rarely been better.

9 SUNDAY
Moon Age Day 9 • Moon Sign Pisces

am..

pm..
As the Moon moves into your opposite sign, prepare yourself for a quieter
day and make the most of what it can offer. There might be certain jobs
to do that you don't care for the look of and it would be sensible to get
them out of the way as early in the day as you can. At least relatives will
help you out.

← *NEGATIVE TREND*									*POSITIVE TREND* →				
-5	-4	-3	-2	-1					+1	+2	+3	+4	+5
						LOVE							
						MONEY							
						LUCK							
						VITALITY							

10 MONDAY

Moon Age Day 10 • Moon Sign Pisces

am ....

pm ....
It would be best to let trusted friends and probably colleagues sort out some of the decisions today, since you are really not in the best frame of mind for doing so yourself. It might feel as if someone does not understand you, though the truth is more likely to be that you are not explaining yourself fully.

11 TUESDAY

Moon Age Day 11 • Moon Sign Pisces

am ....

pm ....
Someone manages to put you in the picture and as a result you are able to make gains that would not have been possible at this time last week. If there is a financial implication to this then so much the better. Probably also a good day with regard to existing friendships and new ones that begin to figure in your life.

12 WEDNESDAY

Moon Age Day 12 • Moon Sign Aries

am ....

pm ....
If you are reluctant to socialise today it is probably only because there does not seem to be sufficient time. Some hours to yourself would be good, though so many other people have a need of you that finding any isolation could seem to be impossible. What you really do not need today are distractions.

13 THURSDAY

Moon Age Day 13 • Moon Sign Aries

am ....

pm ....
As a direct contradiction to the last couple of days you now find yourself better able to come to terms with the needs that others have of you. So much so that you are willing to co-operate with just about anyone and will be likely to make gains as a result. Don't do more than you have to at work however.

14 FRIDAY
Moon Age Day 14 • Moon Sign Taurus

am..

pm..
Some news that you were waiting for may be inclined to let you down.
Try to look at everything as positively as you can and realise that you
have the power to turn almost any situation around at present. The high
esteem that you held in by some people comes as a welcome support in
a general sense.

15 SATURDAY
Moon Age Day 15 • Moon Sign Taurus

am..

pm..
This is a day when you simply have to fall in line, even if this sometimes
goes against the grain a little. You have so many planets in your fourth
house at the moment that you will also notice how very important home-
based matters are inclined to be. Regular routines are inclined to suit
you well now.

16 SUNDAY
Moon Age Day 16 • Moon Sign Gemini

am..

pm..
Being a Virgo subject you are bound to be a fairly complex sort of person,
but you have a real talent at the moment for taking the complexity out
of almost any situation. This means that you are able to come straight
to the heart of any matter and will be almost certain to find this talent
of use personally.

← *NEGATIVE TREND*							*POSITIVE TREND* →			
-5	-4	-3	-2	-1		+1	+2	+3	+4	+5
					LOVE					
					MONEY					
					LUCK					
					VITALITY					

17 MONDAY
Moon Age Day 17 • Moon Sign Gemini

am..

pm..
Whilst domestic issues and family matters generally are tied to eventualities that you have not chosen, there might be little that you can do to change them in any way. Instead you should be concentrating your effort on work matters and will be starting the new working week with a greater sense of purpose.

18 TUESDAY
Moon Age Day 18 • Moon Sign Cancer

am..

pm..
There may not be much relaxation about now, but you can find moments to really be yourself if you are willing to look hard enough. Actually finding the time may be the problem since you are busy in so many directions. It would be wise to take a moment or two to recognise your successes and to enjoy them.

19 WEDNESDAY
Moon Age Day 19 • Moon Sign Cancer

am..

pm..
Venus in your solar fifth house is almost certain to bring a great boost to your love life and allows you to feel that things are going your way personally speaking. Once again you notice attention coming your way, and this is especially true for single Virgoans who might have been on the lookout for love.

20 THURSDAY
Moon Age Day 20 • Moon Sign Leo

am..

pm..
At work you could be rather inactive and unwilling to commit yourself to ventures that look decidedly strange. You certainly will not be talked into anything that does not appeal to you directly and are much more likely than usual to simply sit back and wait to see what happens. Make weekend social plans now.

21 FRIDAY
Moon Age Day 21 • Moon Sign Leo

am ....

pm ....
Unusually, you might be more interested in doing what you want in a social or leisure sense than you are in getting on with your work. Well everyone gets to the stage sometimes when they have to relax a little from pressure and this is simply your time. As a result the weekend should start early for Virgo this week.

22 SATURDAY
Moon Age Day 22 • Moon Sign Leo

am ....

pm ....
A slow start to the day turns into great activity later. The reason is that the Moon is entering your sign of Virgo now and brings with it a desire on your part to catch up on everything that may have been more or less ignored earlier. This turns the week on its head in a way as Saturday becomes a practical time.

23 SUNDAY
Moon Age Day 23 • Moon Sign Virgo

am ....

pm ....
You will have no choice but to realise that this is Sunday, so that no matter how energetic you feel, certain frustrations could hold you back, even if this stems only from the fact that the banks are not open today. Basically though you are in a good position to move forward rapidly on a number of fronts.

← *NEGATIVE TREND*								*POSITIVE TREND* →		
-5	-4	-3	-2	-1		+1	+2	+3	+4	+5
					LOVE					
					MONEY					
					LUCK					
					VITALITY					

24 MONDAY   *Moon Age Day 24 • Moon Sign Virgo*

am..

pm..
Your home life is now much more rewarding than it might have appeared
to be of late. The fact that you start the day with the lunar high still in
your chart does little to prevent you from looking at domestic affairs and
only increases your desire for a happier time. General trends look good,
as do finances.

25 TUESDAY   *Moon Age Day 25 • Moon Sign Libra*

am..

pm..
The ability to think on your feet and to make the sort of decisions that
those around you are less willing to make sets you apart right now. You
won't find yourself in the mood for pushing over any buses in a physical
sense and yet is seems as though you are able to find ways round any sort
of obstacle.

26 WEDNESDAY   *Moon Age Day 26 • Moon Sign Libra*

am..

pm..
You are very likely now to take the leading role in any relationship
situation. It may not be like you to be quite as up front as you presently
seem to be, but the trend is not a bad one at all. Any minor frustrations
brought about as a result of the behaviour of younger people are soon
dispelled.

27 THURSDAY   *Moon Age Day 27 • Moon Sign Libra*

am..

pm..
Because you are willing to sit down and to apply yourself right from the
word go, it is truly amazing just what you can get done. Don't listen to
people who constantly use the word 'can't' and understand that, right
now, it does not occur in your vocabulary. Some fantastic offers should
not be ignored.

28 FRIDAY
Moon Age Day 28 • Moon Sign Scorpio

am...

pm...
Because you still do not allow yourself to be distracted you are able to finish the working week with a real flourish. Someone who you thought was not really on your side turns out to be a supporter of great influence and power. Attention to detail is a piece of cake at the moment and you excel at work.

29 SATURDAY
Moon Age Day 0 • Moon Sign Scorpio

am...

pm...
Don't get involved with the personal situations created by others unless you know that you are definitely not going to get out of your depth. You can afford to relax some of the pressure that you have been applying to your own life, if only for the weekend. Anyone is only capable of doing so much, even a Virgoan.

30 SUNDAY
Moon Age Day 1 • Moon Sign Sagittarius

am...

pm...
The last day of the month and a Sunday to please yourself. December lies ahead, with plenty to do and a great deal to play for in a professional sense. It might be worth a moment or two taken out to realise how much you have achieved of late and to work out how you can build on your general success.

← NEGATIVE TREND						POSITIVE TREND →				
-5	-4	-3	-2	-1		+1	+2	+3	+4	+5
					LOVE					
					MONEY					
					LUCK					
					VITALITY					

1997

YOUR MONTH AT A GLANCE

The twelve numbered boxes represent the important areas in your life. The key to the numbers you will find beneath the panel. A sun above the number indicates that opportunities are around. A cloud below the number, that you should be a bit defensive. Nothing above or below and life will be pretty ordinary.

☀				☀		☀					
1	2	3	4	5	6	7	8	9	10	11	12
	☁					☁					

KEY

1 Strength of Personality	7 One to One Relationships
2 Personal Finance	8 Questioning, Thinking & Deciding
3 Useful Information Gathering	9 External Influences / Education
4 Domestic Affairs	10 Career Aspirations
5 Pleasure & Romance	11 Teamwork Activities
6 Effective Work & Health	12 Unconscious Impulses

DECEMBER HIGHS AND LOWS

Here, I show how the rhythm of the Moon will affect you this month. Like the tide, your energies and abilities will rise and fall with its pattern. When it is above the date line, go-for-it. When it is below the line you should be resting.

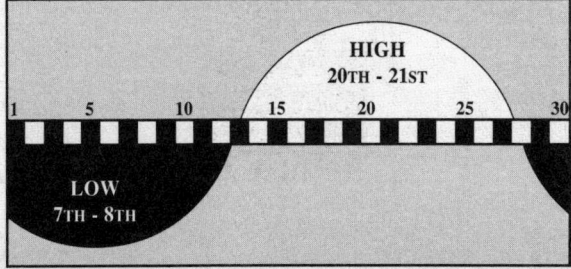

1 MONDAY
Moon Age Day 2 • Moon Sign Sagittarius

am ....

pm ....
Start the day, the week and the month as you mean to go on, and then you will not disappoint yourself or anyone else. Your capacity for simply getting things done has rarely been better than it seems to be at the moment and there is every sensible reason for putting that extra bit of effort in now.

2 TUESDAY
Moon Age Day 3 • Moon Sign Capricorn

am ....

pm ....
Trying to make up your mind whether to concentrate on your home life and the needs it has of you, or on work, forms the biggest part of the conflict within your mind. It ought to be possible to do both, but not if you insist on worrying about things and refuse to take offered advice that you know is wise.

3 WEDNESDAY
Moon Age Day 4 • Moon Sign Capricorn

am ....

pm ....
Your need to be easygoing, light-hearted and cheerful is noticed by just about everyone you come across. Your sense of humour is highly charged at present and there is every reason to believe that you are as popular as ever with friends. You also stand the chance of mixing with some very influential types now.

4 THURSDAY
Moon Age Day 5 • Moon Sign Aquarius

am ....

pm ....
There ought to be some romantic high spots that are very noticeable today. Because you are so able to monitor the way others are thinking you can have a bearing on the way they behave. This could give you a tremendous feeling of power, which needs to be dealt with by a strict look at your motives.

5 FRIDAY   *Moon Age Day 6 • Moon Sign Aquarius*

am..

pm..
Your boredom threshold tends to be very low at present and so you
should try to make certain that something different and stimulating can
happen. Of course you will be busy planning for the festive season and
getting everyone else into the right frame of mind too, but you also need
a more 'now' sort of excitement.

6 SATURDAY   *Moon Age Day 7 • Moon Sign Aquarius*

am..

pm..
You are likely to see both personal and professional matters proceeding
more or less as you would have planned. Misunderstandings are possible
with relatives and you will be doing all you can to keep these to a
minimum, at least early in the day. Confrontation is not a good way to
proceed at present.

7 SUNDAY   *Moon Age Day 8 • Moon Sign Pisces*

am..

pm..
Things hold you back, mainly thanks to the position of the Moon, which
is not at all useful to you at the moment. All you can really do is to cast
your mind forward in time and to make the most of the time that comes
your way to plan. You may find acquaintances to be more useful to you
than you expected.

← NEGATIVE TREND							POSITIVE TREND →				
-5	-4	-3	-2	-1			+1	+2	+3	+4	+5
					LOVE						
					MONEY						
					LUCK						
					VITALITY						

8 MONDAY
Moon Age Day 9 • Moon Sign Pisces

am...

pm...
Patience is of the essence now, mainly because you are not really in the mood to undertake many of the tasks that turn out to be your life at present. You need some time on your own, in order that you can look at things in a less cluttered way than might have been the case for a day or two. Listen to your intuition.

9 TUESDAY
Moon Age Day 10 • Moon Sign Aries

am...

pm...
Christmas apart, this might turn out to be the happiest day of the month. The Sun is especially strong for you at the moment and everything is going your way domestically speaking. At work you have more than enough push and energy to get your own way. What could please a Virgoan more than this?

10 WEDNESDAY
Moon Age Day 11 • Moon Sign Aries

am...

pm...
With a slight sense that life is slowing down, and that there appears to be little you can do about the situation, you may not be exactly on top form today. All the same there is a sort of progress to be made, not least of all in a financial sense. You are planning very carefully and will want to spend wisely.

11 THURSDAY
Moon Age Day 12 • Moon Sign Taurus

am...

pm...
This is a day when you should be willing to trust your intuition to the full and not allow yourself to be diverted by the somewhat dubious advice that comes in from outside. Counting yourself as being quite fortunate financially at the moment, do not be surprised if Lady Luck has a part to play in the proceedings.

12 FRIDAY   *Moon Age Day 13 • Moon Sign Taurus*

am...

pm...
The vulnerable side of your nature is now stimulated by the arrival of
some slightly negative aspects in your solar chart. What you probably
need more than anything is some rest, a commodity that might not be too
easy to come by during a busy day. Social relaxation may be almost as
good.

13 SATURDAY   *Moon Age Day 14 • Moon Sign Gemini*

am...

pm...
Personal and social goals keep you on the move today and anxious to
make the sort of progress that you could feel has eluded you for a while.
There is plenty of support coming in from the direction of your friends,
many of whom are willing to put themselves out on your behalf at a
moment's notice.

14 SUNDAY   *Moon Age Day 15 • Moon Sign Gemini*

am...

pm...
It could seem as if everyone except you is making headway in life, a fact
that can be rather annoying at a time when you take great delight in
showing the world just how capable you are. It is important to look at
things in a long-term sense however and not to allow yourself to be side-
tracked by the immediate future.

← *NEGATIVE TREND*								*POSITIVE TREND* →		
-5	-4	-3	-2	-1		+1	+2	+3	+4	+5
					LOVE					
					MONEY					
					LUCK					
					VITALITY					

15 MONDAY
Moon Age Day 16 • Moon Sign Cancer

am ....

pm ....
You are much more affectionate with loved ones at the moment and will
me more than happy to show them the ropes regarding any aspect of life
about which they are unsure. With all the patience in the world you can
also be a guide and helper at work, where you do what you can to be of
assistance to colleagues.

16 TUESDAY
Moon Age Day 17 • Moon Sign Cancer

am ....

pm ....
An excellent period for entertaining and for getting everyone else to do
the work that is involved. Although you are probably very busy in more
practical ways too, you certainly will not go short of the right sort of
support. Give yourself a great big pat on the back for a success that is
entirely down to you.

17 WEDNESDAY
Moon Age Day 18 • Moon Sign Leo

am ....

pm ....
New social contacts of an important nature can be made at this time and
the possibilities that come about as a result of them turn out to be quite
remarkable. Work and play come in equal measure during the middle
of this week and the balance that you achieve as a result creates a very
rewarding period.

18 THURSDAY
Moon Age Day 19 • Moon Sign Leo

am ....

pm ....
Not everything that is being said at the moment is equally welcomed by
you, and especially not on those occasions when it seems that there are
barbed comments being pushed in your direction. If you have some
important message to get across to a person in authority, get it out of the
way now.

19 FRIDAY

Moon Age Day 20 • Moon Sign Leo

am...

pm...
A family matter brings certain facts to light that you may not really care
for the look of. If this turns out to be the case it would be best not to react
too harshly and to sit back and reflect on matters if you possibly can.
Keep a grip on career issues and don't allow decisions to be taken lightly.

20 SATURDAY

Moon Age Day 21 • Moon Sign Virgo

am...

pm...
Immediately ahead of Christmas week the Moon pays a visit to your sign.
Any last minute details are dead easy to sort out under these trends and
this can turn out to be both a successful and a happy sort of day. Forward
planning is also very important though and possibly rarely more so than
at this time.

21 SUNDAY

Moon Age Day 22 • Moon Sign Virgo

am...

pm...
You show no signs of slowing down at all, and in fact the reverse is
probably true. The only slight word of warning is to remind you of all that
stands before you in a social sense and to advise a little rest in advance
of it. Not that most Virgoans would take all that much notice when they
feel so vibrant.

← NEGATIVE TREND						POSITIVE TREND →				
-5	-4	-3	-2	-1		+1	+2	+3	+4	+5
					LOVE					
					MONEY					
					LUCK					
					VITALITY					

22 MONDAY

Moon Age Day 23 • Moon Sign Libra

am...

pm...
Life is on the move, and just in time for the start of a new working week.
Much of your usual vitality shows and you start to look at longer-term
plans in a more realistic manner than was possible over the weekend.
Refuse to take no for an answer in any situation relating to a social
Christmas.

23 TUESDAY

Moon Age Day 24 • Moon Sign Libra

am...

pm...
Domestic matters should be very rewarding today, even though you
could find that the amount of time that you have to devote to them tends
to be very limited. Everything looks set fair for the sort of organised time
ahead that you relish so much but there could be a detail or two that still
have to be decided.

24 WEDNESDAY

Moon Age Day 25 • Moon Sign Libra

am...

pm...
It is hard on this Christmas Eve to develop any sort of real pattern, or
to get others to behave in a way that satisfies you. Being a little too fussy
in advance of Christmas is quite normal for you and so is nothing that
you would choose to worry over. Act in a determined manner as you finish
work today.

25 THURSDAY

Moon Age Day 26 • Moon Sign Scorpio

am...

pm...
Contacts between the Sun and Venus make this the most interesting of
Christmas Days and particularly so where your love life is concerned.
You have plenty to offer and others really do notice the care you have
taken on their behalf. A particular surprise that you have planned
means that a relative has a good time.

26 FRIDAY
Moon Age Day 27 • Moon Sign Scorpio

am . . . .

pm . . . .
Boxing Day slows you down a little, which may be no bad thing. You can afford to take a little rest and should not think about straying far from home if you have any real choice in the matter. It would be sensible to listen to what younger members of the family have to say at the moment and to act on it.

27 SATURDAY
Moon Age Day 28 • Moon Sign Sagittarius

am . . . .

pm . . . .
Your skill today lies in your ability to get others to do what you want. Having such a good time may well be getting on your nerves a little and it is likely that as a result you will be pushing yourself into some practical directions too. If you don't exactly feel on top form then rely upon a little rest.

28 SUNDAY
Moon Age Day 29 • Moon Sign Sagittarius

am . . . .

pm . . . .
With today comes the need to get out of the house, into the big, wide world that lies beyond your door. You have to be prepared to be sensible, even though you show a definite desire to want to take risks. Only undertake anything really unusual if you find your confidence level high.

← NEGATIVE TREND								POSITIVE TREND →				
-5	-4	-3	-2	-1				+1	+2	+3	+4	+5
					LOVE							
					MONEY							
					LUCK							
					VITALITY							

29 MONDAY
Moon Age Day 0 • Moon Sign Sagittarius

am ....

pm ....
You are probably creating far more impact than you believe and should discover, especially if you are back at work, just how much notice those around you have been taking. You have sown the seeds of ideas in other people's minds and now they should be germinating. The crop that springs up pleases you no end.

30 TUESDAY
Moon Age Day 1 • Moon Sign Capricorn

am ....

pm ....
Expect plenty of help and goodwill from others, and hey presto, it comes your way. A better than average day from all practical points of view, though perhaps somewhat less good when it comes to dealing with one-to-one relationships. You can at least turn on the charm when it proves to be necessary, though effort is required.

31 WEDNESDAY
Moon Age Day 2 • Moon Sign Capricorn

am ....

pm ....
The last day of the year and you are likely to make it one that you will remember for a long time. All the same you have your thinking head on and will be certain to view the coming period with a sense of certainty and confidence. It might not be possible to get as many details sorted out as you would wish.

← *NEGATIVE TREND*						*POSITIVE TREND* →			
-5	-4	-3	-2	-1	+1	+2	+3	+4	+5
LOVE									
MONEY									
LUCK									
VITALITY									

RISING SIGNS
for VIRGO

Look along the top to find your date of birth, and down the side
hour (or two) if appropriate for Summer Time.

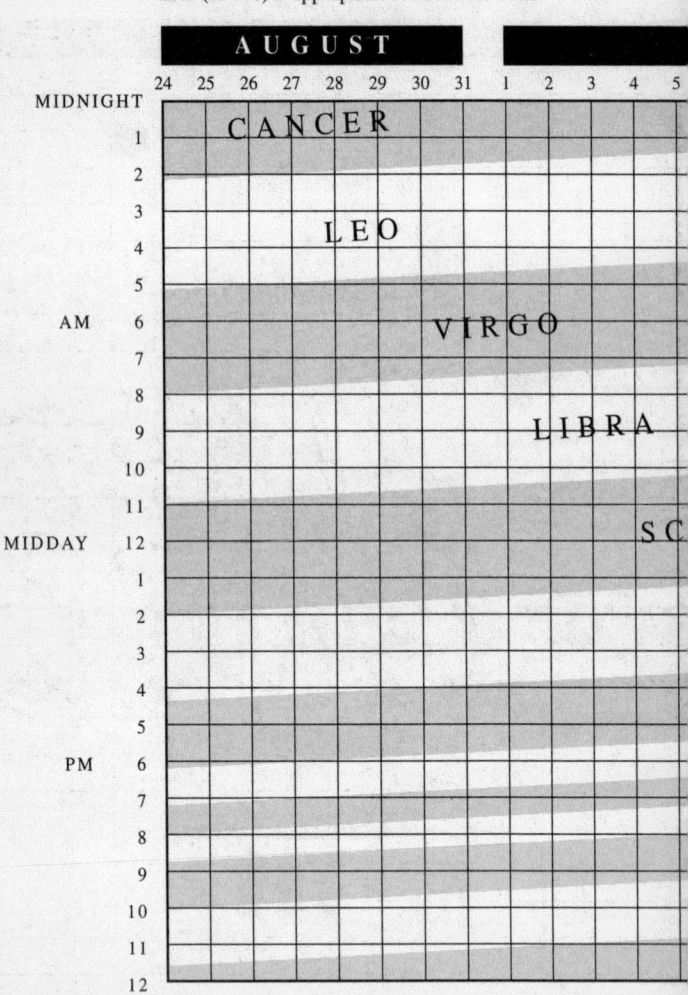

	AUGUST											
	24	25	26	27	28	29	30	31	1	2	3	4	5

MIDNIGHT
1 — CANCER
2
3
4 — LEO
5
AM 6 — VIRGO
7
8
9 — LIBRA
10
11
MIDDAY 12 — S C
1
2
3
4
5
PM 6
7
8
9
10
11
12

ur GMT birth time. Where they cross is your Rising Sign. Don't forget to subtract an

| 7 | 8 | 9 | 10 | 11 | 12 | 13 | 14 | 15 | 16 | 17 | 18 | 19 | 20 | 21 | 22 | 23 |

0
1
2
3
4
5
6
7
8
9
10
11
PIO
12
1
SAGITTARIUS
2
3
CAPRICORN
4
5
AQUARIUS
6
PISCES
ARIES
7
TAURUS
8
GEMINI
9
10
CANCER
11
12

THE ZODIAC AT A GLANCE

Placed	Sign	Symbol	Glyph	Polarity	Element	Quality	Planet	Glyph	Metal	Stone	Opposite
1	Aries	Ram	♈	+	Fire	Cardinal	Mars	♂	Iron	Bloodstone	Libra
2	Taurus	Bull	♉	−	Earth	Fixed	Venus	♀	Copper	Sapphire	Scorpio
3	Gemini	Twins	♊	+	Air	Mutable	Mercury	☿	Mercury	Tiger's Eye	Sagittarius
4	Cancer	Crab	♋	−	Water	Cardinal	Moon	☽	Silver	Pearl	Capricorn
5	Leo	Lion	♌	+	Fire	Fixed	Sun	☉	Gold	Ruby	Aquarius
6	Virgo	Maiden	♍	−	Earth	Mutable	Mercury	☿	Mercury	Sardonyx	Pisces
7	Libra	Scales	♎	+	Air	Cardinal	Venus	♀	Copper	Sapphire	Aries
8	Scorpio	Scorpion	♏	−	Water	Fixed	Pluto	♇	Plutonium	Jasper	Taurus
9	Sagittarius	Archer	♐	+	Fire	Mutable	Jupiter	♃	Tin	Topaz	Gemini
10	Capricorn	Goat	♑	−	Earth	Cardinal	Saturn	♄	Lead	Black Onyx	Cancer
11	Aquarius	Waterbearer	♒	+	Air	Fixed	Uranus	♅	Uranium	Amethyst	Leo
12	Pisces	Fishes	♓	−	Water	Mutable	Neptune	♆	Tin	Moonstone	Virgo

THE ZODIAC, PLANETS
AND CORRESPONDENCES

In the first column of the table of correspondence, I list the signs of the Zodiac as they order themselves around their circle; starting with Aries and finishing with Pisces. In the last column, I list the signs as they will appear as opposites to those in the first column. For example, the sign which will be positioned opposite Aries, in a circular chart will be Libra.

Each sign of the Zodiac is either positive or negative. This by no means suggests that they are either 'good' or 'bad', but that they are either extrovert, outgoing, masculine signs (positive), or introspective, receptive, feminine signs (negative).

Each sign of the Zodiac will belong to one of the four Elements: Fire, Air, Earth or Water. Fire signs are creative and enthusiastic; Air signs are mentally active and thoughtful; Earth signs are constructive and practical; Water signs are emotional and have strong feelings.

Each sign of the Zodiac also belongs to one of the Qualities: Cardinal, Fixed or Mutable. Cardinal signs are initiators and pioneers; Fixed signs are consistent and inflexible; Mutable signs are educators and live to serve.

So, each sign will be either positive or negative, and will belong to one of the Elements and to one of the Qualities. You can see from the table, for example, that Aries is a positive, Cardinal, Fire sign.

The table also shows which planets rule each sign. For example, Mars is the ruling planet of Aries. Each planet represents a particular facet of personality – Mars represents physical energy and drive – and the sign which it rules is the one with which it has most in common,

The table also shows which metals and gem stones are associated with, or correspond with the signs of the Zodiac. Again, the correspondence is made when a metal or stone possesses properties that are held in common with a particular sign of the Zodiac. This system of correspondences can be extended to encompass any group, whether animal, vegetable or mineral – as well as people! For example, each sign of the Zodiac is associated with particular flowers and herbs, with particular animals, with particular towns and countries, and so on.

It is an interesting exercise when learning about astrology, to guess which sign of the Zodiac rules a particular thing, by trying to match its qualities with the appropriate sign.

The News of the Future

In the Almanack

Racing Tips — All the Classics. Dozens and dozens of lucky dates to follow — for Trainers and Jockeys.

Football and Greyhounds too.

Gardening Guide — Better Everything. Bigger; better; more colour. Whatever you want! Lunar planting is the key.

Fish Attack — Anglers get the upper hand and catch more fish. Dates, times and species to fish are all here.

With Key Zodiac Sign dates of course.

A great New Year investment for you.
An inexpensive, fun gift for your friends.

Look for it at W. H. Smith, John Menzies, Martins and all good newsagents.

Free Gift WORTH £8.00

1997 IS MY ANNIVERSARY - 300 YEARS!

It really is quite remarkable that I have been able to sustain so many loyal readers for so long. As one of them I thank you most sincerely.

In fact I would like to offer you a Free Gift to celebrate our long friendship.

The gift I have chosen is a highly polished Gilt Pendent, on its own fine chain. It will carry what I regard as the most powerful Talisman for *luck, happiness and improvement*.

The Medal will be cast by the regalia manufacturer who is by **Royal Appointment to Her Majesty the Queen** and I am sure you will be delighted by the very high quality of my gift.

All I ask of you is that you pay the cost of your Postage, Packing & Storage Box for which my Publishers have asked £2.00.

This is a GENUINE offer. This item normally costs £9.99 by Mail Order. Unfortunately I can allow only one gift per book and this offer must close January 31st 1997.

"Old Moore"

How To Apply for Your Privileged Reader's Gift.

1) You may only apply once using the Reservation Form above.
2) Write your name and address in Block Capital Letters on the above Application Form and send it with a cheque or P. O. for just £2.00 payable to BJA, to : PO BOX 361, SLOUGH, SL1 5YT.
3) Demand will be heavy, so you may have to wait for up to 28 days.